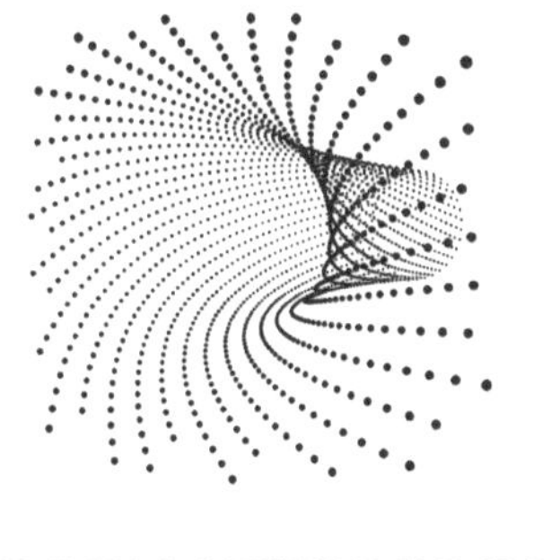

FIRSTMATTERPRESS

Portland, Ore.

OUR FAVORITE PEOPLE IN THE ROOM

literary/art anthology

FIRSTMATTERPRESS

Portland, Ore.

First Edition

Published in the United States
by First Matter Press
Portland, Oregon

Paperback ISBN-13: 978-1-958600-07-8

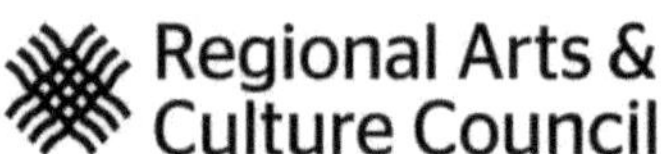

This literary arts project was funded by Regional Arts
and Culture Council's Arts3C Grant Program for
Creation, Cultivation & Community in the Portland
metropolitan tri-county region. www.racc.org

Special thanks to EcoTrust for hosting our 2022
Poetry Scramble through an event space grant.
www.ecotrust.org

Editor: ash good, Lauren Paredes & Emily Moon
Contributing Editors: Hailey Spencer

Cover Illustration
Copyright © 2023 by Lara Rouse
@good_luck_lara

Book design by ash good
ashgood.com

CONTENTS

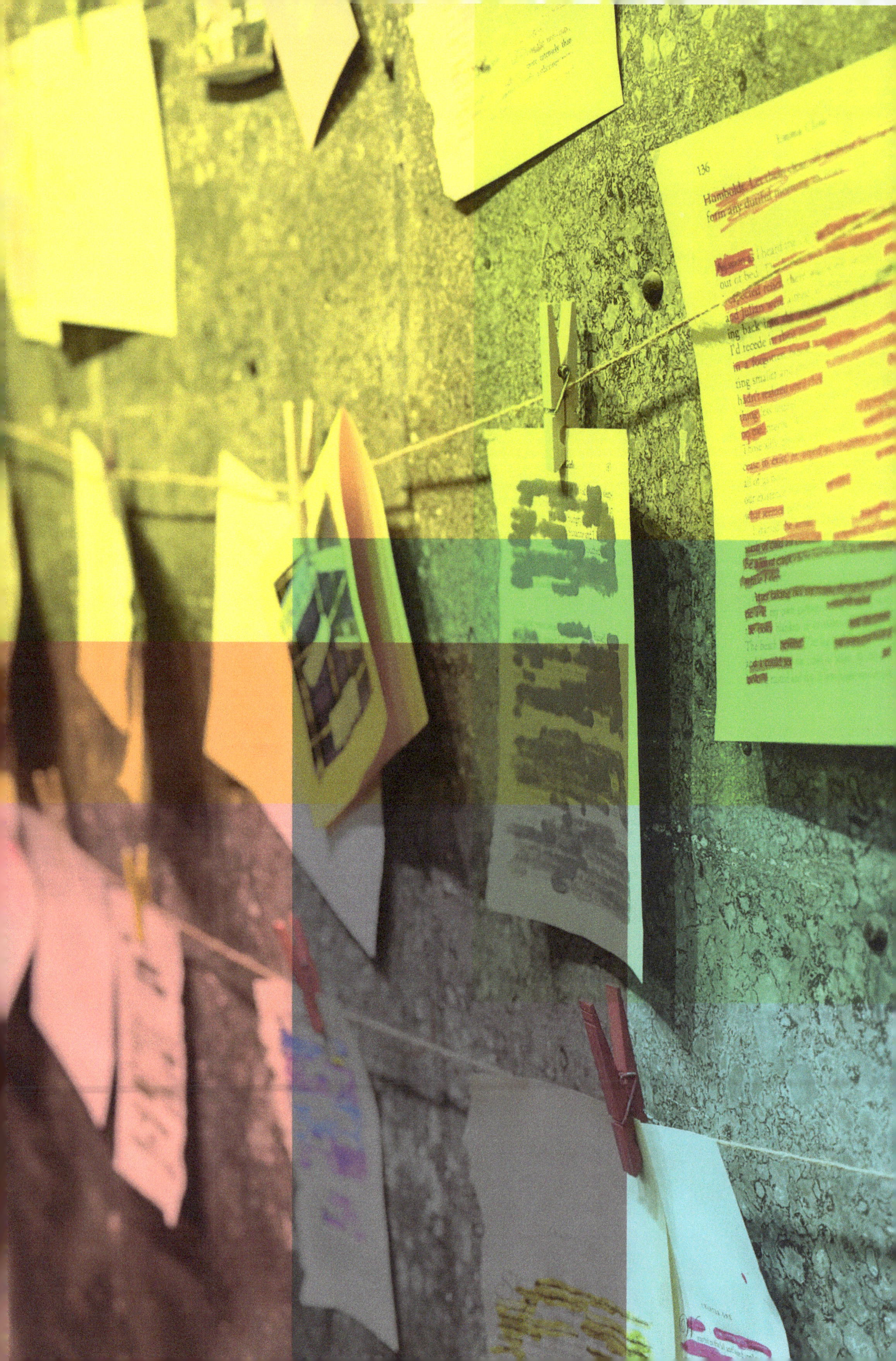

EDITORS' INTRODUCTION: WHEN OUR FAVORITE PEOPLE ARE IN THE ROOM, LANGUAGE BECOMES PLAYGROUND

Last winter, we brought Poetry Scramble to life—an active space of accessible poetic play. Our inaugural Literary Arts' Cover to Cover stop shook things up, inviting writers and non-writers alike to dive into poetry-making stations, team up with neighbors, snag stamps to fill their event passports, and proudly pin their creative gems to our vibrant sharing wall brimming with Human Magnetic Poetry, Mad Libs-style madness, Exquisite Corpse surprises, and more. One of our artist friends said it was the perfect introvert/neurodiverse party where no one had to look anyone else in the eye. And still, there was a warm feeling of community in the space as we created meaning and poetic objects together.

In 2018, the cofounders of First Matter Press were looking around at each other, wondering why the craft-diligent, prolific poets in our Portland workshop group weren't publishing books. We wanted to see our friends at readings and book signings and featured at book festivals. It seemed like a problem we could solve, and a heck of a party we wanted to host. And that August we did just that, releasing our first two titles to a small crowd in a Central Eastside artist's loft.

First Matter Press began by asking: What if it weren't so difficult for first-time and/or experimental PNW writers to find a publishing home? This idea birthed our press named after *prima materia*, the starting material for alchemical reaction that is all around us just waiting to be harnessed. In the past six years, we have published 20 books of poetry and hybrid works.

From a fresh poetic voice learning to bloom as an autistic person to a genre-expanding collage novel that heals through the reordering of intergenerational trauma, we've

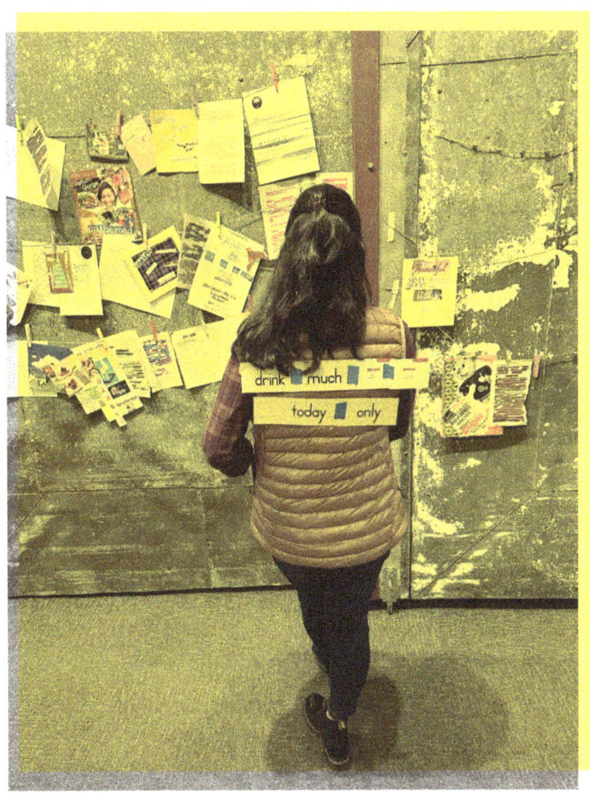

6 WAYS TO PLAY

ERASURE, *a.k.a. Blackout poetry, transforms existing text into a new poem through reduction. In this ekphrastic technique, you'll selectively erase words from a chosen page. Embrace creativity in erasing (using markers, pens, or paint)—there's no single 'right way.' To spark your process, choose a text page at random. Keep rows of five or fewer words consecutively to form an original thought, avoiding repetition of the source. For inspiration, explore works like 'A Humument' by Tom Phillips, 'Hotel Almighty' by Sarah J. Sloat, 'A Little White Shadow' by Mary Ruefle, or 'Even the Air, Too Heavy' by Riley Danvers.*

COLLAGE POETRY *is a fun spin on Surrealist art and is all about spontaneity. Choose words and images you like, toss them on your 'canvas' (blank paper), and see what magic happens. You're creating cool combos and stories. And hey, Surrealists were into rebellious vibes too! So: Get your canvas (blank paper) and adhesive. Cut out words and images you dig. Arrange 'em into a poem—as much or as little as you want. Admire your genius.*

HUMAN MAGNETIC POETRY *is an embodied take on magnetic fridge poetry. Grab word cards, tape 'em on yourself, and whip up a haiku or a snappy short poem. Need an emergency word? Blank cards got you covered. Feeling social? Team up with pals! Everyone tapes cards for a line or phrase, then arrange yourselves for a complete poem. Feeling fancy? 'Twister' it up with creative taping and positioning—no rules here, we made up the game!*

MAD LIBS-STYLE POEMS *are inspired by Xylophone Mykland's poem 'SadLibs.' Fun fact: In 1953, Leonard Stern and Roger Price cooked up Mad Libs, but they couldn't agree on a name. Five years later, at NYC's Eggs Benedict spot, they overheard an actor and agent clash. Actor wanted to 'ad-lib,' agent said 'mad.' Voilà! 'Mad Libs' was born in '58. Usually for stories, we invite you to take your fave poems and, in the spirit of Mad Libs, swap nouns, verbs, adjectives—go wild! Grab a pal, and boom, you've got a wacky, teamwork-packed piece!*

helped elevate emerging PNW authors who write from an immediacy of experience. Over the years, we have built a cohort model that engages editors and authors in reflective, horizontal collaboration, which we believe is essential to nurturing literary craft. As an added and enriching layer, we also foster the intersection of literature and art by pairing author cohorts with local featured artists to collaborate on bespoke cover art.

Thriving literature communities hunger for contributions from both respected and fresh names. Alchemizing prima materia among our writing peers is valuable, necessary work. Opening the world of poetic play to the young and/or non-writer public feels equally vital and indispensable.

The multi-modal nature of poetic language engages our cognitive functions, stimulating neural activity and contributing to brain growth and development. Through its emotional resonance, imaginative engagement, language processing demands, and meaning-making challenges, poetry offers a unique and enriching experience that nurtures the brain's capacity for creativity, empathy, and critical thinking.

In times that yearn for revolutionary healing and new ways of being, poetry serves as a conduit for collective consciousness, captures the spirit of change, and gives voice to the aspirations and frustrations of people. By tapping into the emotional, cultural, and imaginative dimensions of human experience, poetry plays a crucial role in igniting, sustaining, and guiding our world-building.

Playing with language can be a social activity that fosters connections. Shared laughter over wordplay or linguistic jokes can create a sense of camaraderie and strengthen relationships. Experimenting with language helps individuals become more attuned to linguistic nuances, enhancing their ability to communicate effectively. This skill is particularly useful when engaging with diverse audiences or navigating complex conversations.

This collection documents a selection of the creative works generated at Poetry Scramble and features new work from 16 of our legacy editors, authors, and artists.

If this anthology, our 20th book, has found its way into your hands, we hope it serves as an inspirational primer into the many playful forms poetic exploration and communal storytelling can embody. May you be moved to write. To collaborate. To play.

—ash good, Lauren Paredes & Emily Moon
Editors

EXQUISITE CORPSE *is a collab game invented by Surrealists. Think of it like a quirky mix of 'Telephone' and 'Consequence'—hope for some wild twists and heartfelt moments. Here's the deal: Take turns writing lines to craft a poem. Trick is, you only see the line just before yours. Start by snagging a line from any poem as the opener. Read, write below, then fold so the next player sees only your line. Next person writes, folds—repeat! Last lines? They're kinda special. Remember that if you're wrapping it up. When the page is packed, unfold and see what the gang's cooked up!*

CENTO *comes from Latin, meaning 'patchwork.' It's like sewing different pieces into a cool poetic outfit. Poets borrow lines from others to create something fresh and generate new meanings by juxtaposing borrowed lines in new ways. The cento form has been around forever, used by poets worldwide to remix language, spark conversations, and make new magic by blending old lines.*

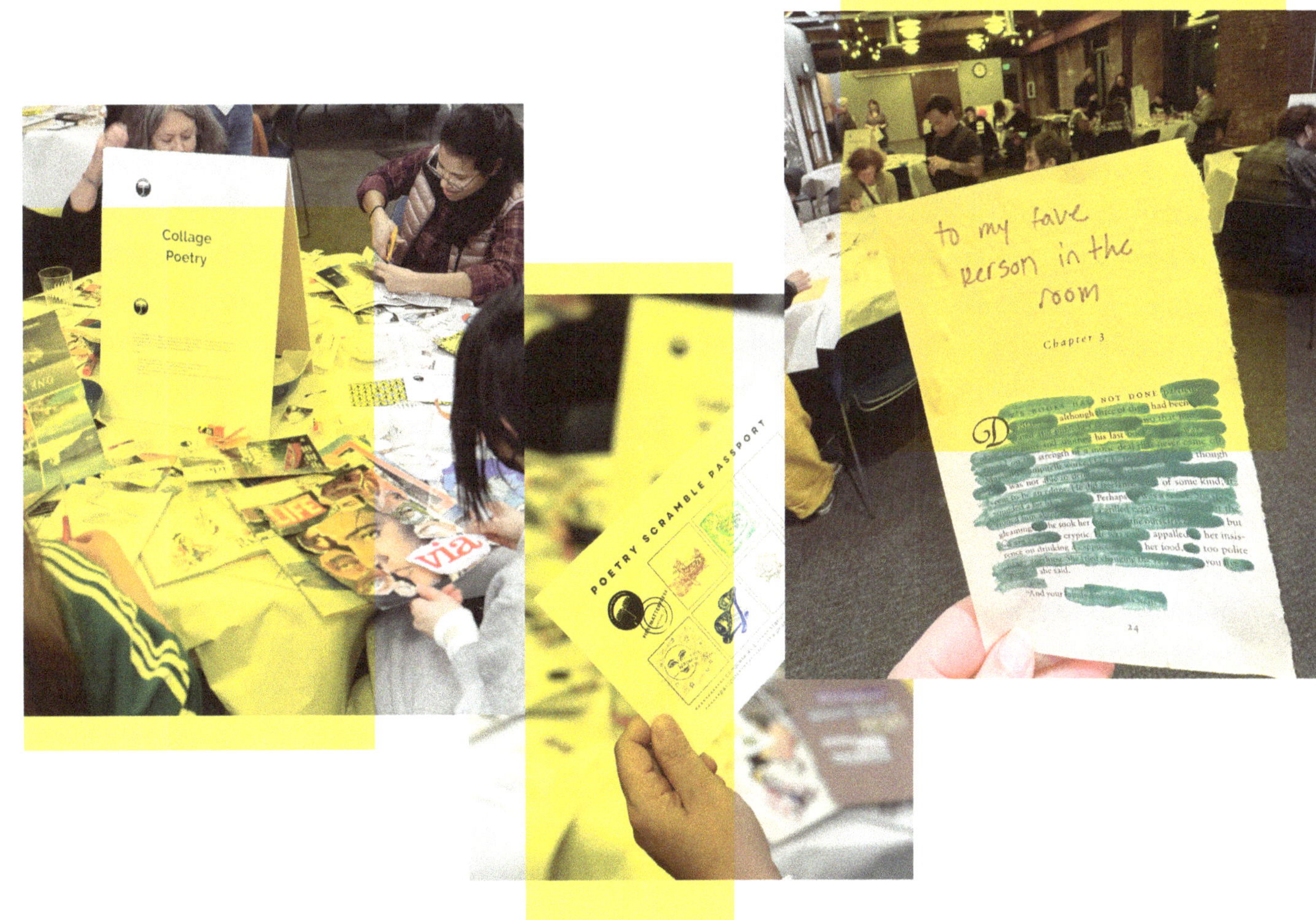

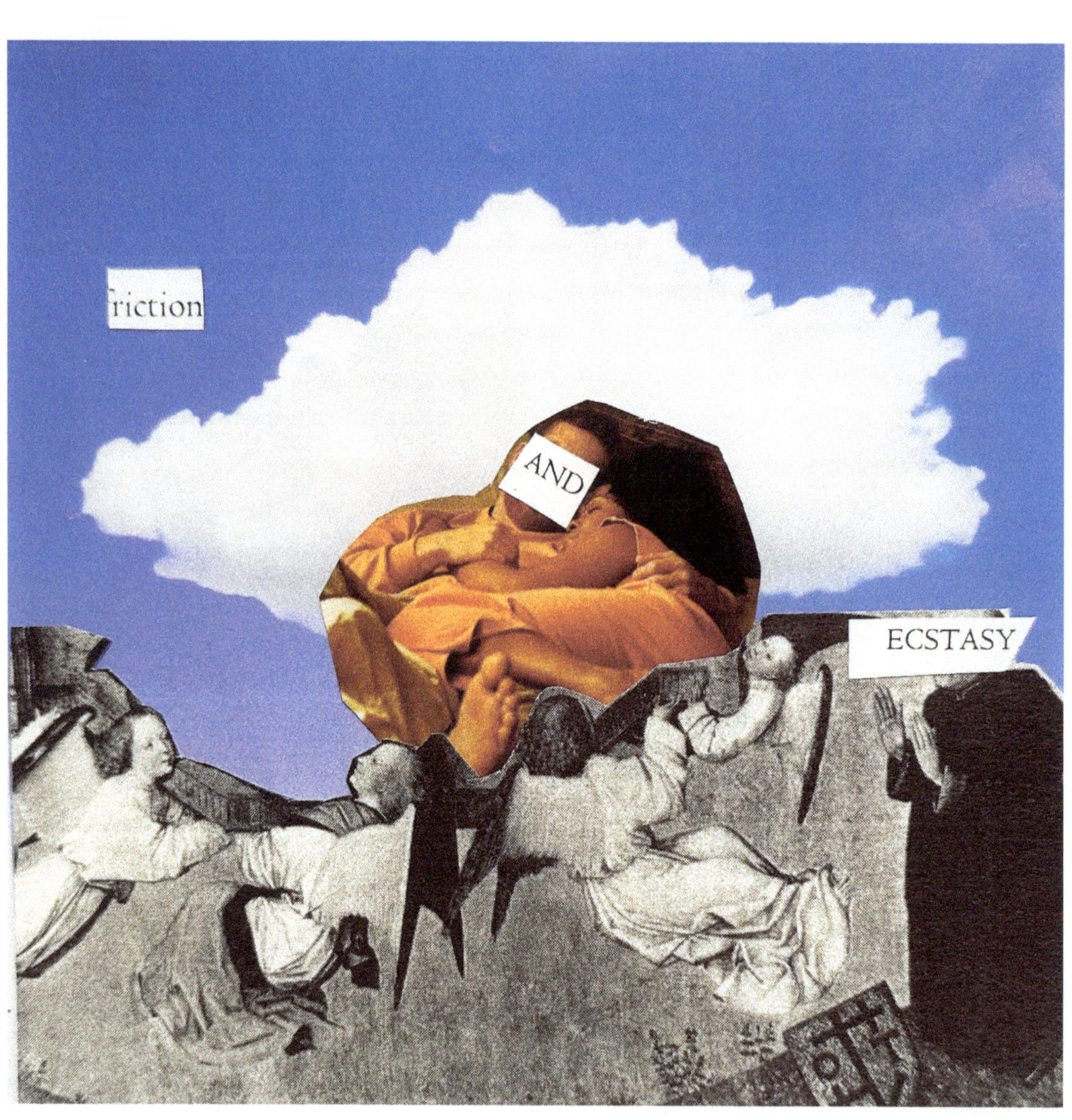

COLLAGE created by community members on Nov. 4, 2022 at First Matter Press's *Poetry Scramble*.

I stumble on the step of my brain's dark staircase

recover to find dust in the corners

"Dusky, the coroner said, "You are now known as Ashes."

but the old lady was still laying on the hotel room
floor
and when she woke up she blurted:
I am an invisible creature

blind like a sunlit worm
feeling the sun like an inner light
But the light fades away second by second
and the night takes center stage

EXQUISITE CORPSE written by community members on Nov. 4, 2022 at First Matter Press's *Poetry Scramble*. Starting line "I stumble on the steps of my brain's dark staircase" was excerpted from *Someone I Can Hold Gently* by Xylophone Mykland (First Matter Press, 2022).

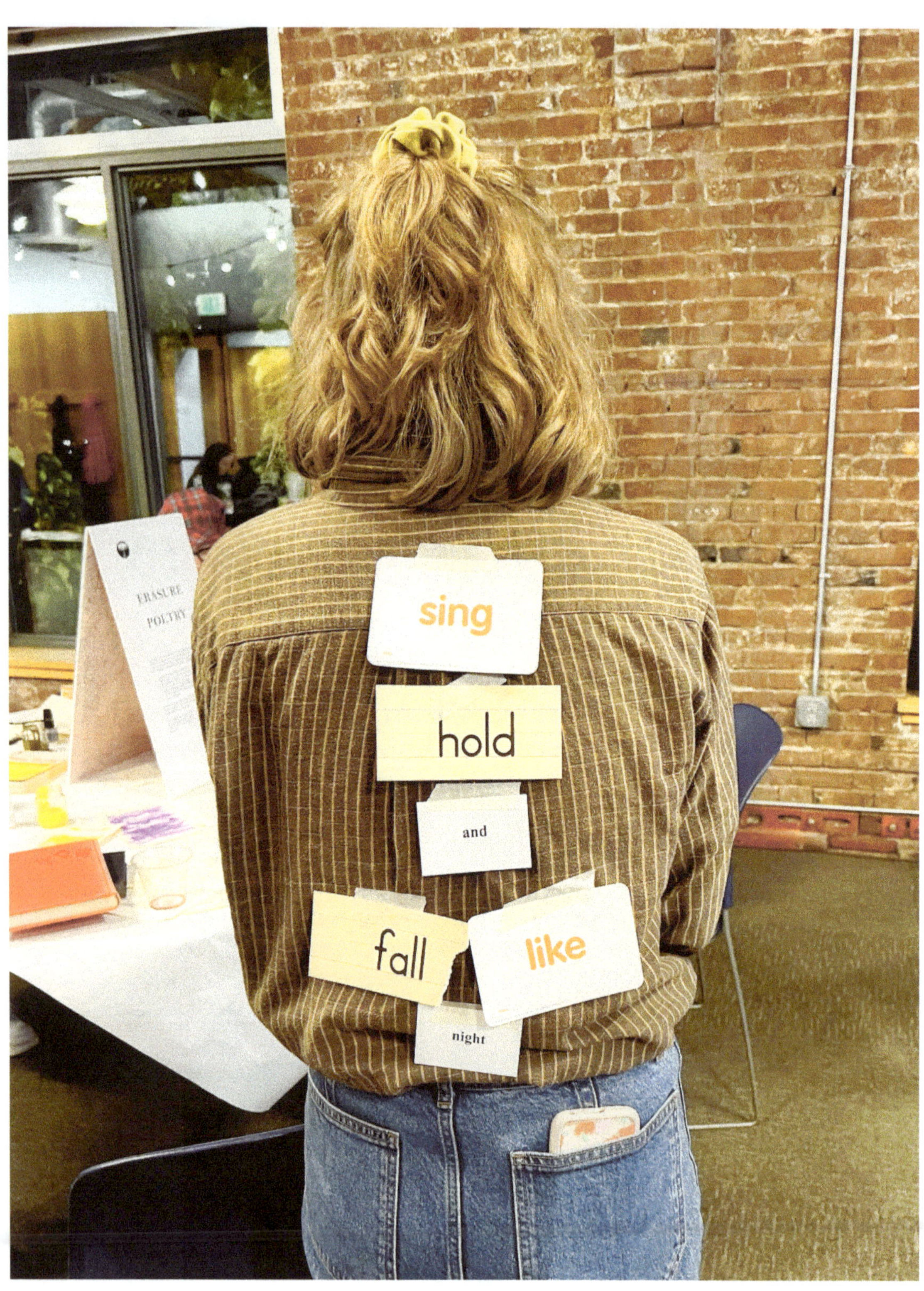

HUMAN MAGNETIC POETRY created by community members on Nov. 4, 2022 at First Matter Press's *Poetry Scramble*.

THE NIGHT PARADE

The night parade _____Shakes_____ swiftly spinning
VERB ENDING IN -S

a _____Salsa_____ like needle work. Lovers and other
TYPE OF DANCE

still creatures come _____Savor_____ it slip down
VERB

_____Lovejoy_____, between swirling trees, lifting
PORTLAND STREET NAME

their _____hats_____. The night parade plays trumpets,
TYPE OF CLOTHING

cymbals, drum, _____Signaling_____, longing, hypnotic
ADJECTIVE ENDING IN -ING

_____Xylophone_____ that tumbles over our faces, covers the spine
MUSICAL INSTRUMENT

and _____ribcage_____ of the tarmac. It sweeps
BODY PART

the city's every part, _____Shielding_____ it like
VERB ENDING IN -ING

a(n) _____wing_____, gently rubbing away its _____Scales_____.
NOUN   NOUN

AFTER PLUCKING STARS

rae diamond

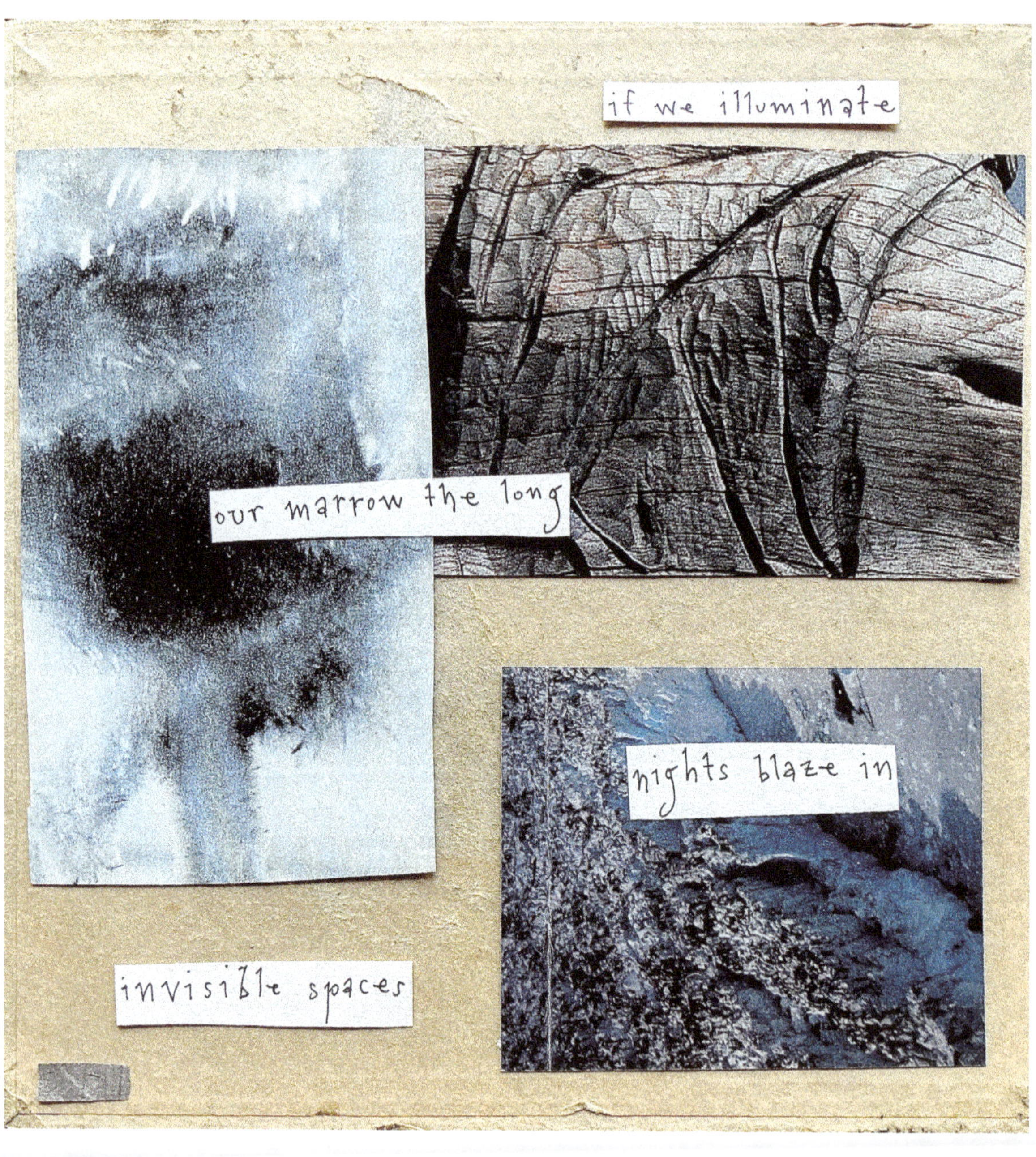

SOVEREIGN

rae diamond

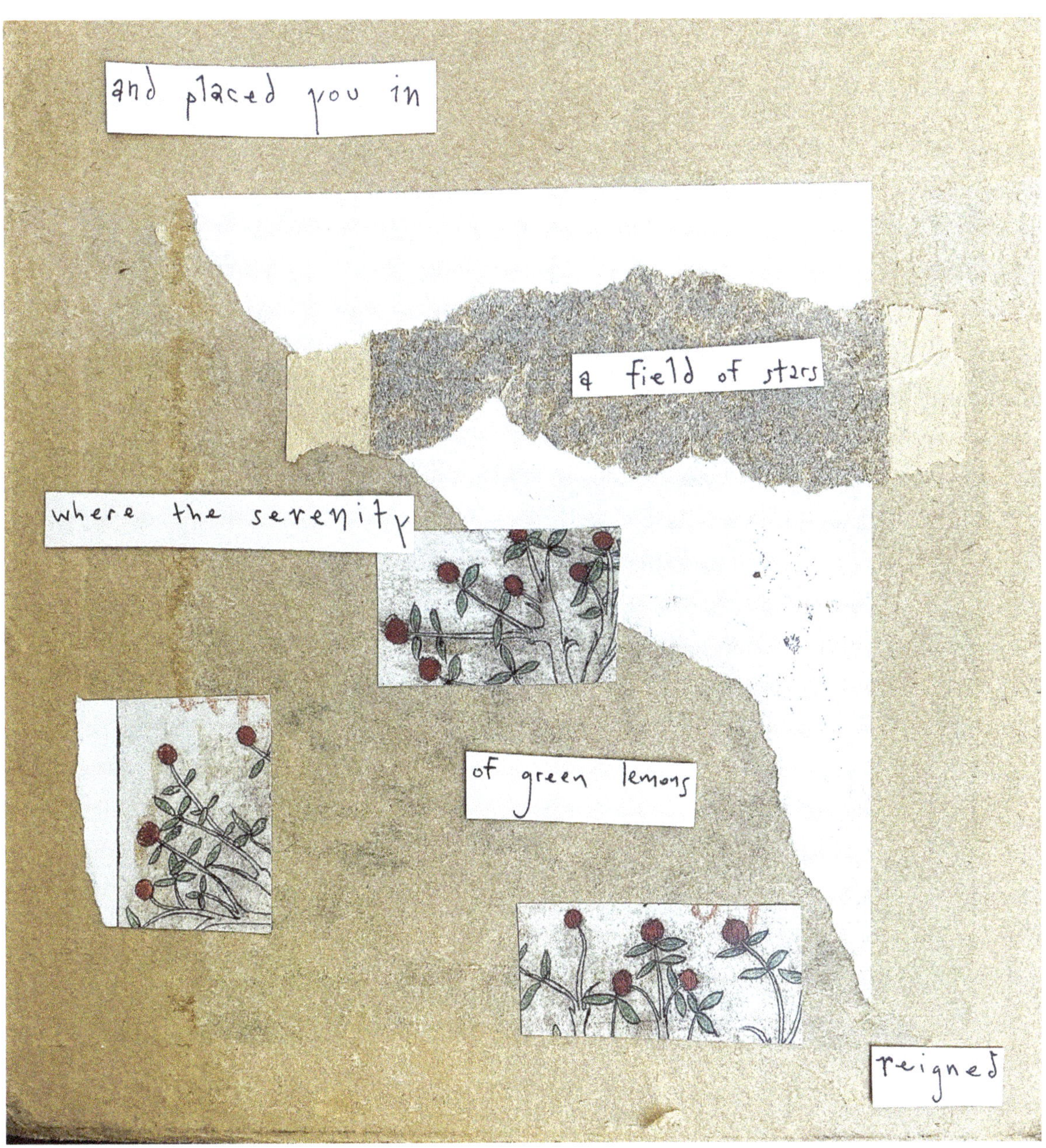

RAE DIAMOND is a neurodivergent interdisciplinary artist, educator, and nature advocate. They wrote, collaged, and published zines as a homeless youth in the '90s, and their poems now appear or are forthcoming in *Petrichor*, *BlazeVOX*, *Clockhouse*, *Miracle Monocle*, and *Sinister Wisdom*. Rae is the author of the prose book, *The Cantigee Oracle* (North Atlantic Books), the founder of the Long Tone Choir, and a lifelong student and teacher of Qigong. Find her online at raediamond.com and @rae13diamond

YIN/YANG

Could you take the spilt *Buttermilk*
LIQUID

with you? Tell me once and for all

if you believe in *Ferment*. Do you have time
NOUN

to clear *26* years' worth of *tables*?
NUMBER · **PLURAL NOUN**

My voice is the black *giraffe* I'm no longer afraid of.
ANIMAL

Are our many *Children* the silver lining?
PLURAL NOUN

There's a shadow in the *Living room* with your *pinky toe*.
ROOM IN A HOUSE · **BODY PART**

For a moment I almost asked you to *transcend*.
VERB

Just before you leave, please tell me—

what is the real *dodecahedron* of letting go?
SHAPE

MAD LIBS-STYLE POETRY created by community members on Nov. 4, 2022 at First Matter Press's *Poetry Scramble*. "Yin/Yang" is from *Otherwise, Magic* by Lauren Paredes (First Matter Press, 2019). Mad Libs-style poems were inspired by "Sad Libs" in *Someone I Can Hold Gently* by Xylophone Mykland (First Matter Press, 2022).

ATTACHMENTS

sonya woehletz

Exhibit A: Mirror

The person who configures herself as a machine to be stapled to a doorway, cross-wise, and discretely, like a small counter, will consider the number of times other bodies may enter and exit. They derive themselves fully in front of a flat surface that, like the slender machine itself, is neither crystal nor fluid.

Exhibit B: Symptoms

I am not talking right now about the way one body responds to the introduction of the other body (albeit much smaller in scale) into its visage, but rather the diffuse vectors of influence that arise without considerable provocation. It only takes a small disturbance, and, as I will have you note, even the most tedious precautions will not forestall a reaction once it has begun.

Exhibit C: Surveillance

A decision begins to sprout in the salt flat of what will one day be a forest. Nobody foresaw that this would happen, or had even imagined that this would unfold over the course of the next million years or so with the most astonishing results. For even amidst the unparalleled extension of a pale horizon into the unfeathered skin of its own consequence, it has been observed that small shoots of resistance are extracted by their roots for the resolute satisfaction of a few stable $NaCl$ ions. Yet, the seedlings invariably grow back. They express no curiosity about the fact of themselves, such considerations remaining beyond the range of species activity. And you see, there is just no way to keep pace with their proliferation. Think of it this way. If one plans to desecrate an entire forest of aspen, then one really must take into consideration the fact that a single aspen organism may extend for miles below the horizon of the observable universe. The logic encoded therein is encased with a sort of membrane of girlhood, knowable always to the adult men in the building, but never to the girl, until it is too late.

Exhibit D: Declension

This time the phone rings. It regresses, as it once did, along the axis of a tense kind of boredom. You smile, and pick up. Someone informs you that your car's extended warranty is about to lapse.

Exhibit E: Expirated

In order to remove the special object placed on the shelf, you must acknowledge what you, yourself, intended to accomplish with this mistake. It is there, in its place, after all. And you are not where you had informed us you would be at this hour.

Exhibit F: Reagents

The undersigned acknowledges the aforementioned and agrees, both as pretext and as condition, to plot out carefully where the stakes will be nailed when the rains flush the ground with NO3- come Friday. The lability of the fleeting regret will prevent any permanent solution. But an attempt at appearances—yes. This can coincide with larger objectives; their positive and negative charges. The electrons will always comply when congratulatory remarks are applied with gentle force. Leaves sprout on the tongue of this agreement. They unfurl themselves in Roman numerals. Pages and pages.

Exhibit G: Form

Not Letters: Numerals: content: Satiated: The revolution of nothingness: Conventions of notation: 0.

Certifications and Representations

On this, the first Friday of In-Ordinate Time, I hereby declare that________________ is both a particle and a wave, and affirm with the present that the invisible Equation No. KXXIVI (also referred to in Exhibit B as "body") has demonstrated it to be true, and I myself confirm my participation in its invisibility as accords with the bonds of my office. The blooming of this admission does not feel immediately special, but I have come to accept that I have responsibility for any and all momentary indecisions, their immediate and long-term sequelae. Within three-weeks' time, all of the naves will have extrapolated their position in relationship to the nearest violence. I only measure the distances between them.

SONYA WOHLETZ was born as a bat in a cave in New Mexico territory. Having since transformed into a human, she now enjoys the use of opposable thumbs to write, paint, cook, and make glorious messes. Her work has appeared in *Latin American Literary Review, Revolute,* and *Roanoke Review,* among others. Sonya's debut collection, *Bir Sira Sonra / One Row After,* was published by First Matter Press is 2022.

Galileo timed the swings with his pulse, and in this way, he verified his observation. Actually, today we know that, if the arc is unusually large, the time is not the same as for a small arc. But you can certainly say that the time is very nearly the same. It is almost perfectly identical if the angles are less than about 10°.

Galileo found that the material of the bob has no effect on the timing, nor does the weight. What matters is the *length* of the pendulum. A long pendulum beats more slowly than a short one. A pendulum four times as long as another takes two times as long to make a beat.

Galileo figured out how to make such a constant-time pendulum activate some gears in order to produce a clock. About fifteen years later Christian Huygens (1629-1695) followed through with these ideas and made the first successful pendulum clock, such as we use even today.

In working with his pendulum, Galileo used it to measure a person's pulse. Thus, he made a valuable medical instrument, even though he was really on his way to pure science and had turned away from a career in medicine.

Galileo ran out of money and had to leave the university, but his scientific work went on, even more intensely than before. He appeared at numerous scientific gatherings to report on his findings. Everyone could see that here was a

I want to learn how to hear with my body

all of the neuropathways and their struggles
-places we've already walked before
golden green in the silvery light
she is still all elbows

forcing me out of the bed at midnight
to wake with a hovering shadow
at the cusp of your vision

EXQUISITE CORPSE written by community members on Nov. 4, 2022 at First Matter Press's *Poetry Scramble*. Starting line "I want to learn how to hear with my body" was excerpted from *One Row After/Bir Sira Sonra* by Sonya Wohletz (First Matter Press, 2022).

UNTITLED COLLAGE

charity e. yoro

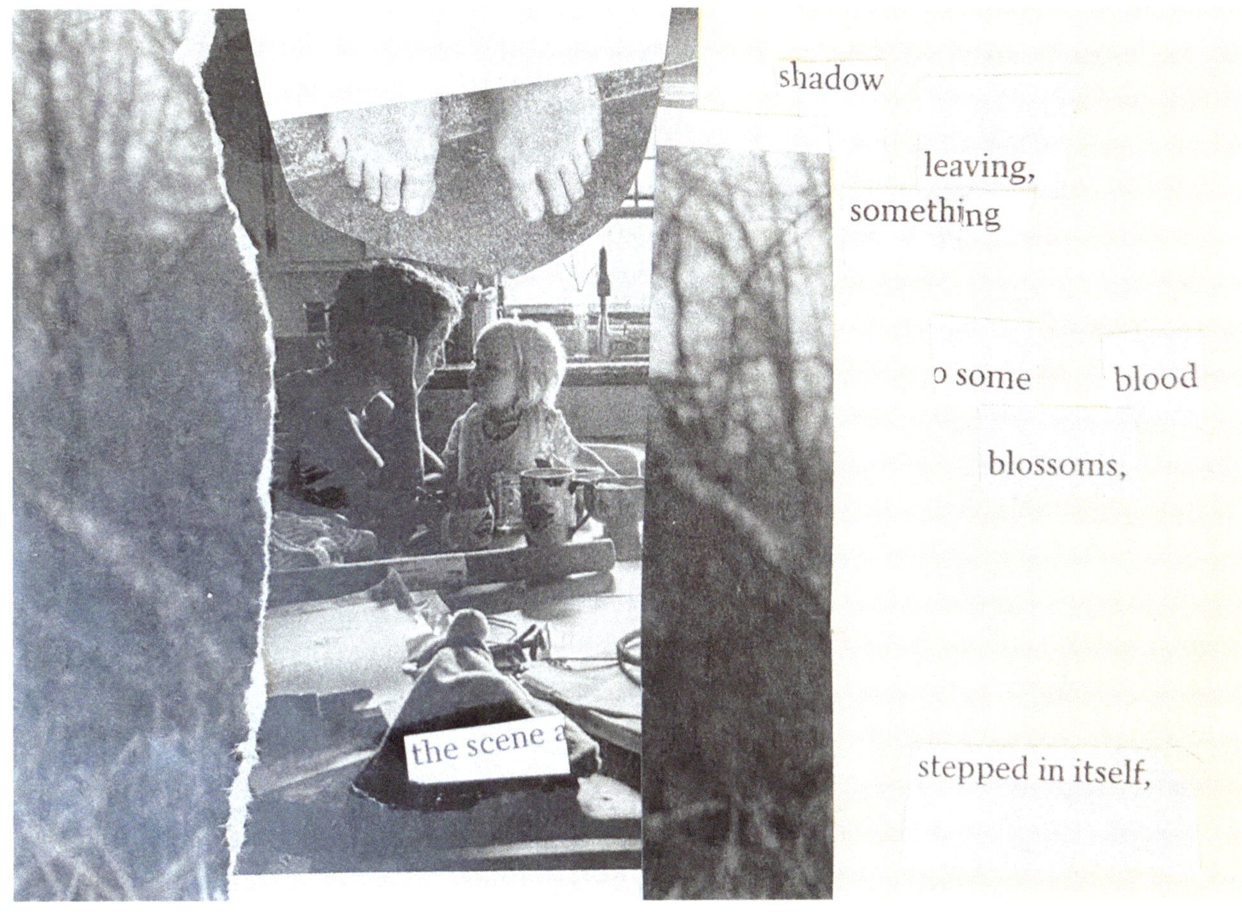

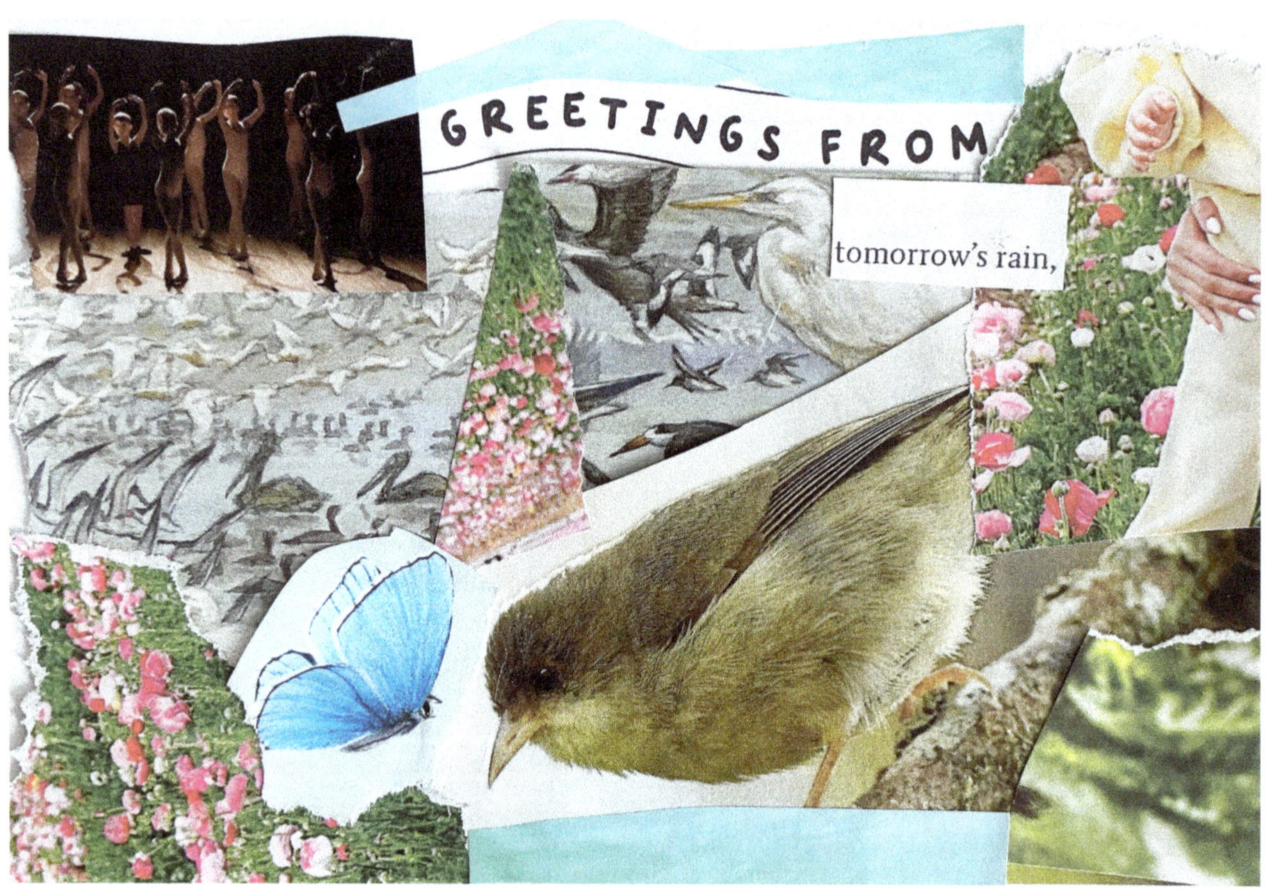

CHARITY E. YORO is a steward of words and beings. Since publishing her first broody poem in 8th grade, her writing has appeared in the *New York Times*, *The Rumpus*, *poets.org*, *Tupelo Quarterly*, and elsewhere. Born, raised, and educated on the east side of O'ahu, she currently lives in Portland, Oregon with her wild, loving family.

HATCH

lauren paredes

beings, were held not to exist, so there was nothing for them to observe or react to, no matter *what* was going on. She had actually heard Marcy Beggs's mother referring to a maid's becoming "uppity, forgetting her place." It had seemed to Jimmie so quaint a phrase that she'd wanted to laugh. Well, if you knew about things like that—servants not knocking on doors—you'd have to say the world had progressed some. Nobody these days, no matter how rich and important, nobody, not even the Beggs family, could get away with pretending that somebody who worked for them didn't exist and couldn't react. That was the sort of thing her mother ought to concentrate on once in a while, instead of on everything that was wrong with society. Not that that was such a great leap forward, or anything, but just the same they hadn't stood *still* in those times. We've advanced a *little*, Jimmie thought.

They went into the study that smelled of pipe tobacco and wood and glue. Dad had a big desk on which he put his carving things. He made, with his thin gifted fingers, marvelous little creatures of wood. Tiny birds to hang on the boughs of a Christmas tree, their little feathers miraculously distinct, each bird painted with a minute delicate brush in bright clear colors. He was carving a chess set now.

"Look at the king," said Jimmie, picking it up. "Isn't he imposing?"

The king—no way of knowing yet if he was the black king or the white, since, as her father said, the painting of this chess set lay far in the future—was six inches tall and he sat upon a throne. Jimmie didn't think there was

63

Of "Hatch (Erasure 37)": Back in 2018, while I was working on my chapbook manuscript for First Matter Press, I was also beginning an erasure poetry practice that helped me settle my mind each night before falling asleep. It was the grounding counterpart to my traditional poems' other (more desperately searching for answers) voice. I went back into my archive to see what I made the week my chapbook came out in March 2019 and was grateful to find Erasure 37 (now titled "Hatch")—it speaks so much to the phase of my life then, a fresh portal for our author cohort, and the press at large, still young and emerging at that time.

FLOWERS FOR THE DEAD

lauren paredes

Some days I wake up with so much honey
in my third eye for you. I try to transmit
the sweetness through a visceral memory,
but it clogs the control panel of the time-
machine. It turns our tether a slow gold.

LAUREN PAREDES is a storyteller across mediums with a soft spot for the unusual. Her work has appeared in *Salamander*, *TRNSFR*, *Warm Milk*, *phoebe*, and elsewhere. Her first chapbook of poems, *Otherwise, Magic*, was released in 2019 by First Matter Press. She currently resides in the Berkshires, nestled between hills.

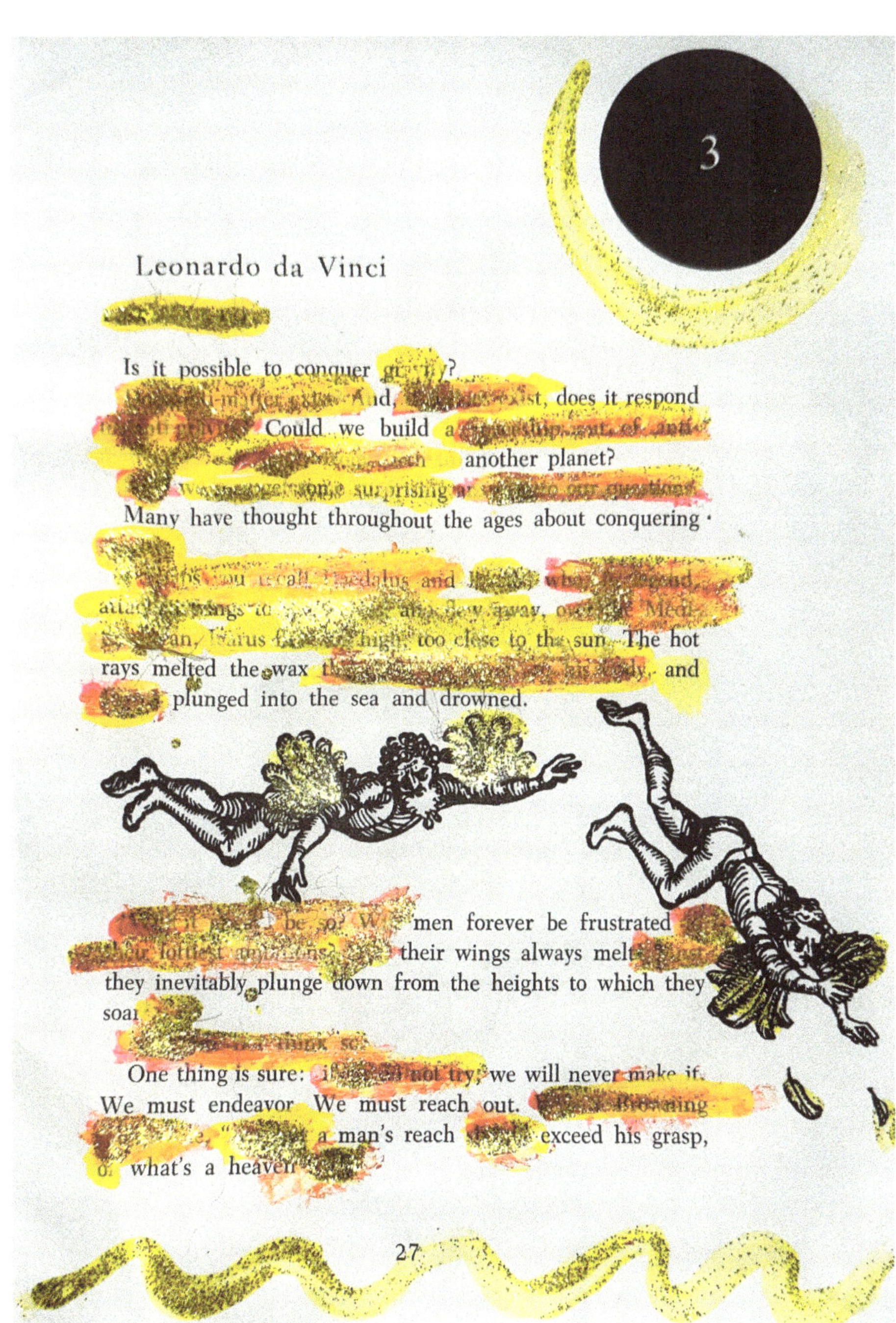

3

Leonardo da Vinci

Is it possible to conquer gravity? And, does it respond Could we build a another planet? surprising Many have thought throughout the ages about conquering

attach wings to and fly away, over the Med Icarus flew too high, too close to the sun. The hot rays melted the wax and plunged into the sea and drowned.

men forever be frustrated their wings always melt they inevitably plunge down from the heights to which they soar

One thing is sure: we will never make it. We must endeavor. We must reach out. a man's reach exceed his grasp, or what's a heaven

27

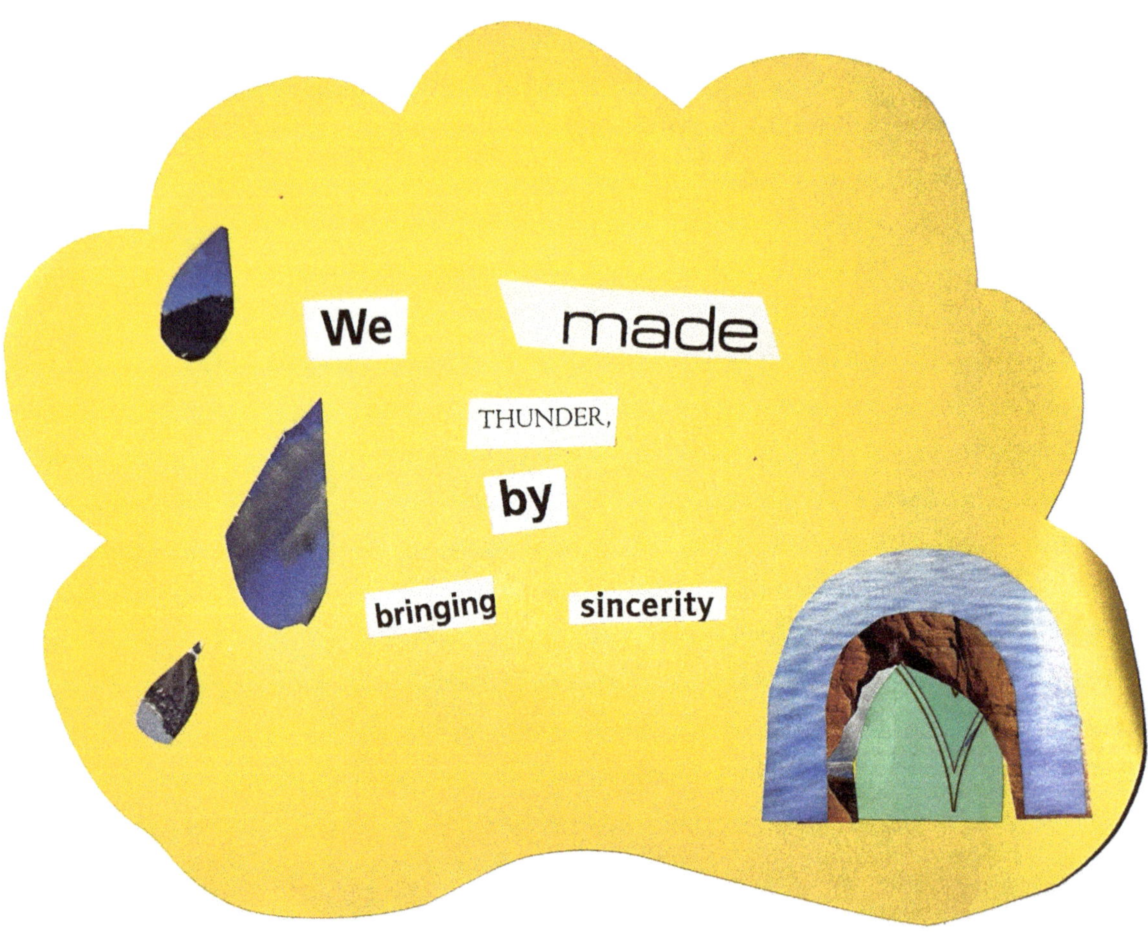

COLLAGE created by community members on November 4, 2022 at First Matter Press's *Poetry Scramble* (a Literary Arts' Portland Book Festival Cover to Cover event).

UNTITLED COLLAGE

lara rouse

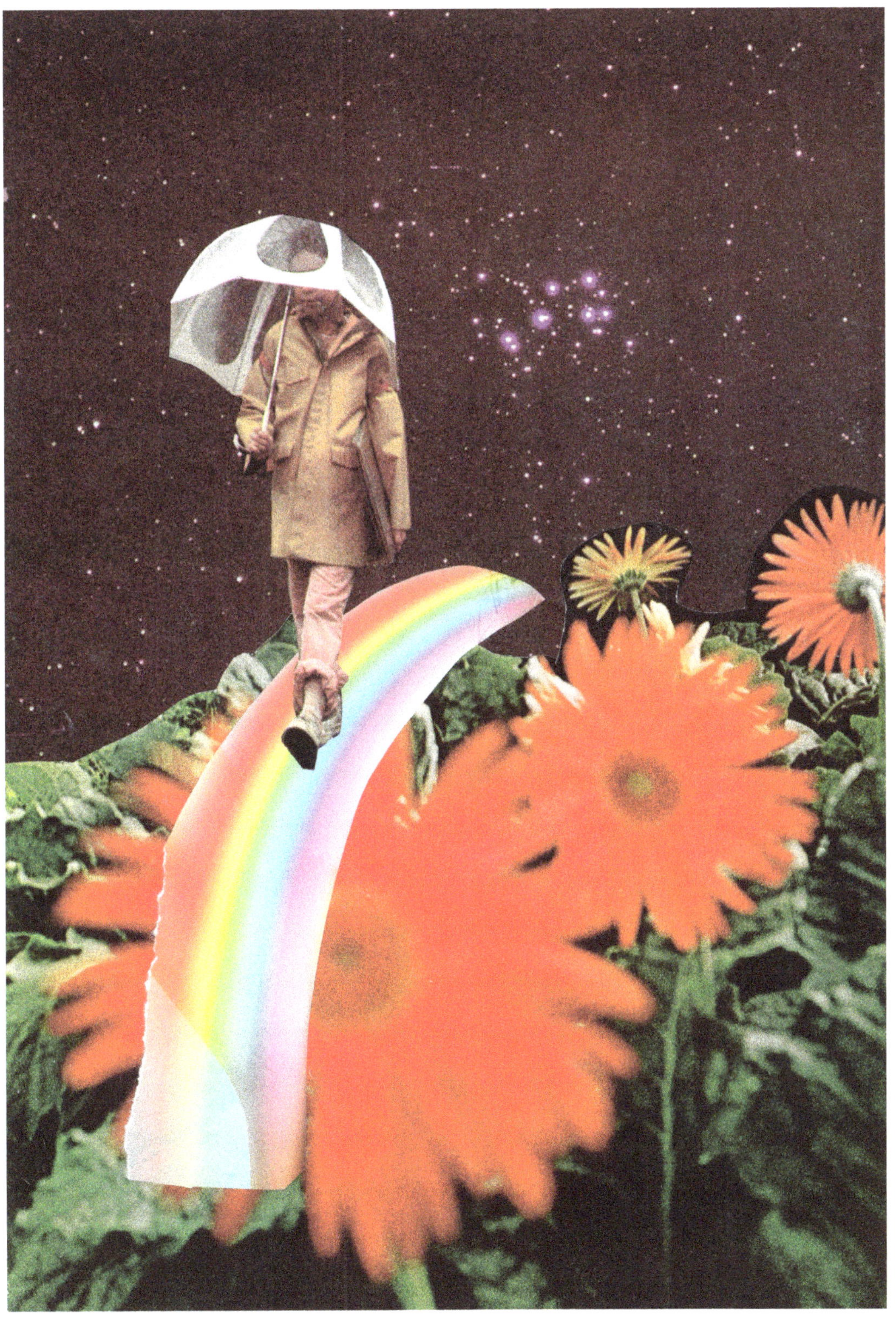

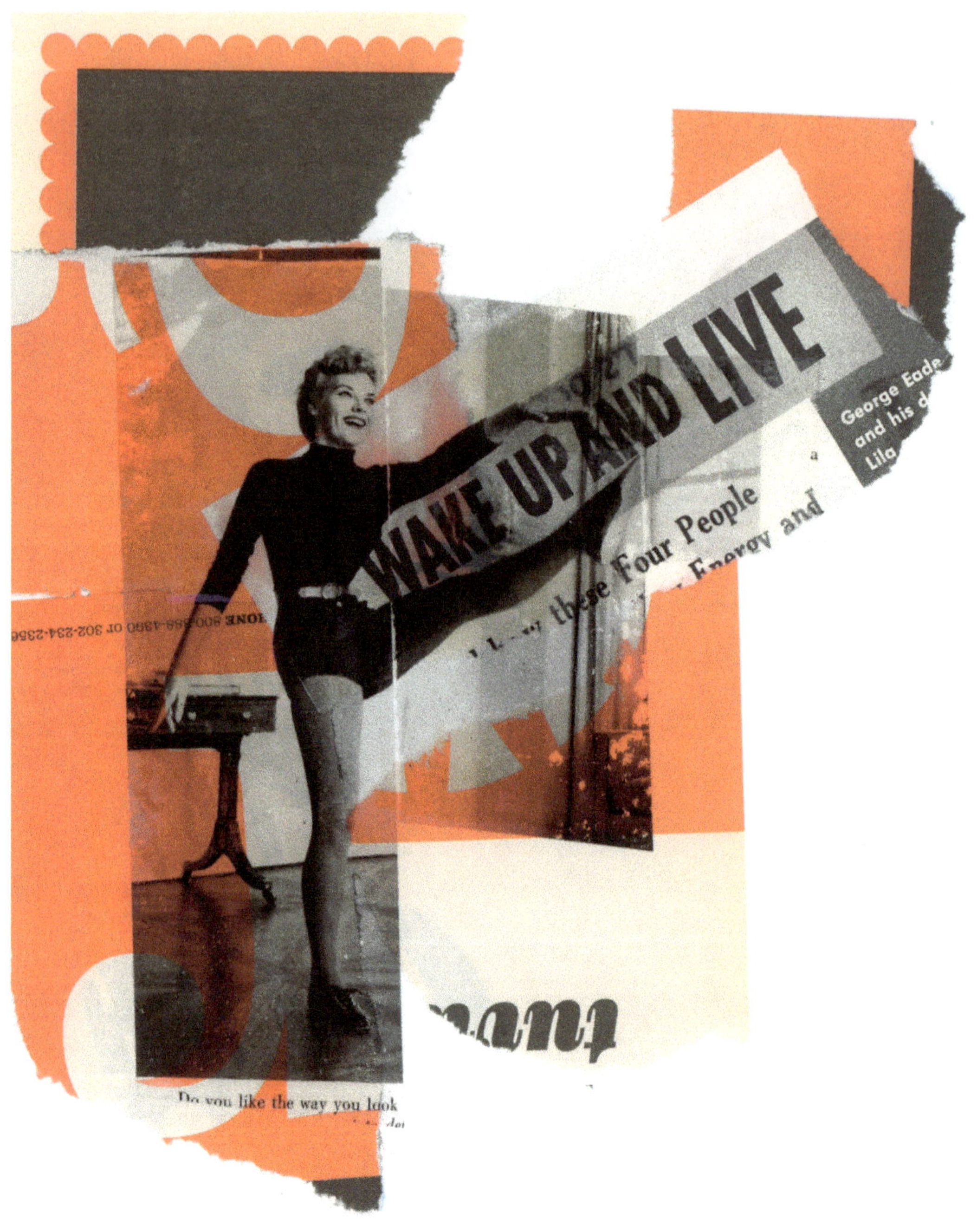

Of "Untitled Collage": *The collages I make are surreal and sometimes abstract. In a way, I'm at the mercy of the source material. It's very difficult for me to make a collage with a specific vision or subject in mind, and this constraint has freed me to make so much more than I could ever have imagined. With these pieces of paper I can control everything. I can forget about the rest of the world for a moment and be peaceful. I am fascinated with music and its ability to transport the listener to a different time and space, and I feel transported when I see a beautiful collage. Collage is beautiful. There would probably be no collages without music. I try not to think when I make collages. It's nice to make collages with music or a podcast on in the background and this helps me not over think what I'm doing. The main things I allow myself to consider are colour palette and balance. The fun and accessibility of collage making keeps me making new art. Before I collaged I painted. Before I painted I drew pictures and was into acting. I always knew it was more of a matter of declaring myself to be an artist. Sometimes I forget and my daughter will tell me, "You're an artist!" And I'm like, "Yes! Yes I am!" I never wanted to do anything else.*

LARA ROUSE is a collage artist living in Portland, Oregon. She makes art for fun and along the way she makes art for friendly people in need of album art or a book cover. Lara was First Matter Press's featured cover artist in 2023.

A FLUID'S GUIDE TO INTERACTING WITH STRANGERS

andra vltavín

Wake up
        put on an outfit
        your mother would say
        doesn't match   Search
the mirror
for a piece of yourself—add color

Decide how long
you'll be interacting with strangers—
binders can only be worn
for 8-10 hours
        and you need two weekdays off
        to breathe

Going to work?
Lower your voice
so you don't get *ma'am*-ed
at the register

Smoking helps—cracks
and scratches are sultry   Plot twist—
cannabis blocks covid
for extra protection
(don't bother with lipstick
when you're wearing
a mask)

Ask yourself what's more inappropriate:
a packer without a binder or
a binder without a packer
        and do it anyway   Test
algorithms to see if they can spot
a female nipple inside a male one

Take your shirt off
at every possibility

Expect confusion   Get a piercing
to remind yourself what permanent
feels like   Water down a waistcoat

unless you're feeling fancy
(refrain from the British accent)

Don't make eye contact on the bus
except with other fluid strangers

Shrug but pop your collar   learn
several songs well enough
to lip-sync   have more favorites
than you can list
so your answer changes daily

Notice who pays attention   who
doesn't recognize you   who gets
angry   *She, he, they, ze, fünf,*
                 sex, sieben, acht   What
did you learn first: numbers
or pronouns?

Have an embarrassing childhood memory
at the ready to prove your identity

Make sure your vaccination card
is free of your dead name
          but whisper it like a spell
          in the dark   Never forget
how to disappear
(wear red if you want to be seen)

Emphasize sunken cheeks
but add concealer
to sunken eyelids—fatigue
doesn't have a gender   Dress

up what makes you happy

Eat with irreverence
          and wear your legs like accessories

Stand on tip-toes   lean in

          and ask your most vulnerable self
          to dance

ANDRA VLTAVÍN (formerly K. M. Lighthouse) is the author of *Body Until Light*, *Time Counts Backward from Infinity*, and two chapbooks of poetry. They have been published in many journals, including *Toasted Cheese*, and were a winner of the 2021 DiBiase poetry contest. They live the revolutions of queerness, creative reuse, and polyamory with their wife, two bunnies, and a spinning wheel in Portland, OR.

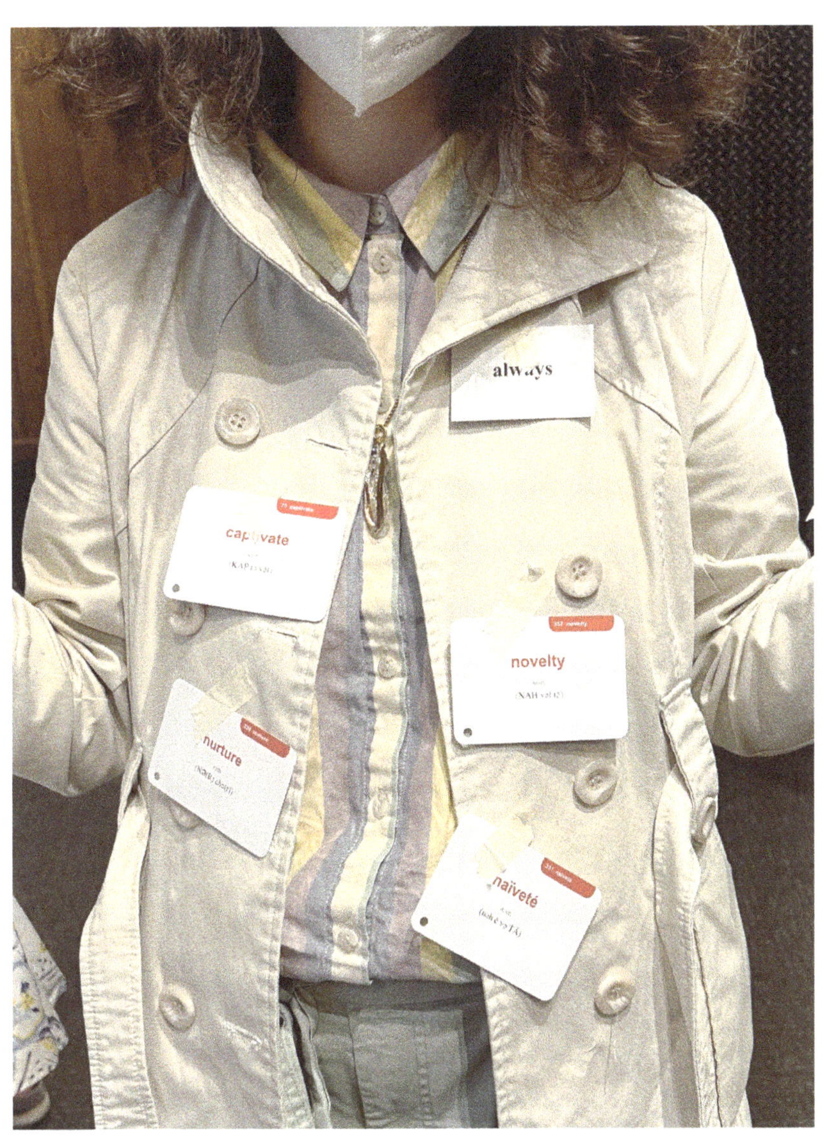

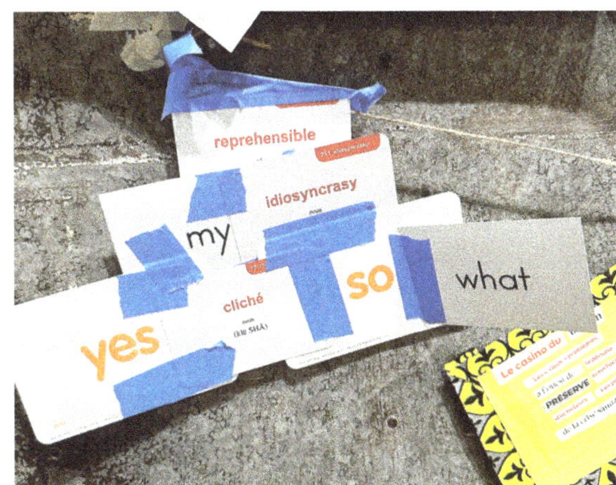

HUMAN MAGNETIC POETRY created by community members on Nov. 4, 2022 at First Matter Press's *Poetry Scramble*.

Bacon doesn't sizzle when it burns

But my mother's skin shed delicate locks
I want to keep them as proof she existed
the unsung proof of the son's gifted bourbon
a scent embedded in warm memory
   like childhood but happier
adulthood but faster
A quintessence of adolescence,
such an awkward time in ones life
our future selves look on w/ amusement
and wonder what the hell happened to honesty.

EXQUISITE CORPSE written by community members on Nov. 4, 2022 at First Matter Press's *Poetry Scramble*. Starting line "Bacon doesn't sizzle when it burns" was excerpted from *Someone I Can Hold Gently* by Xylophone Mykland (First Matter Press, 2022).

C O N F E S S I O N

xylophone mykland

last night I dreamt I fell in love with someone else
in a room filled with worshippers.
I asked if you were jealous & you did the same, vice versa;
if I were awake I would have said no
and lied to us both.

my eyes are house fire in the morning.
I smother them for the rest of the day,
and for the first time in two weeks,
no rain blesses us.

I think the worst emotion to have while writing is shame.
every line I write is three shovelfuls of dirt above the truth,
so here is what I'm afraid of:

I check my phone for your texts like a zealot
who can't control their fervor for something more.
when you fuck me and I say *oh God,*
I'm always slightly embarrassed to say something so close to the truth.
I look in the mirror and say *I can fix you.*
I pray to my vibrator—*please be enough for me.*

there are so many sins I want to confess,
but you forgive me before I can say them.
look at me with your blistering eyes,
tell me about your belief in me, again, again, again.

I push my fingers in your mouth to suck & swallow,
and I find my faith at the ridge where your tongue becomes throat.
you are always meaner to me in my head.

XYLOPHONE MYKLAND (they/them) is a nonbinary lesbian poet and self-proclaimed special occasion, currently based in Portland, OR. When they're not writing poetry, you can find them Googling "androgynous outfits," walking dogs, applying for public assistance, and thinking about poetry. Their debut collection, *Someone I Can Hold Gently,* was published by First Matter Press in 2022.

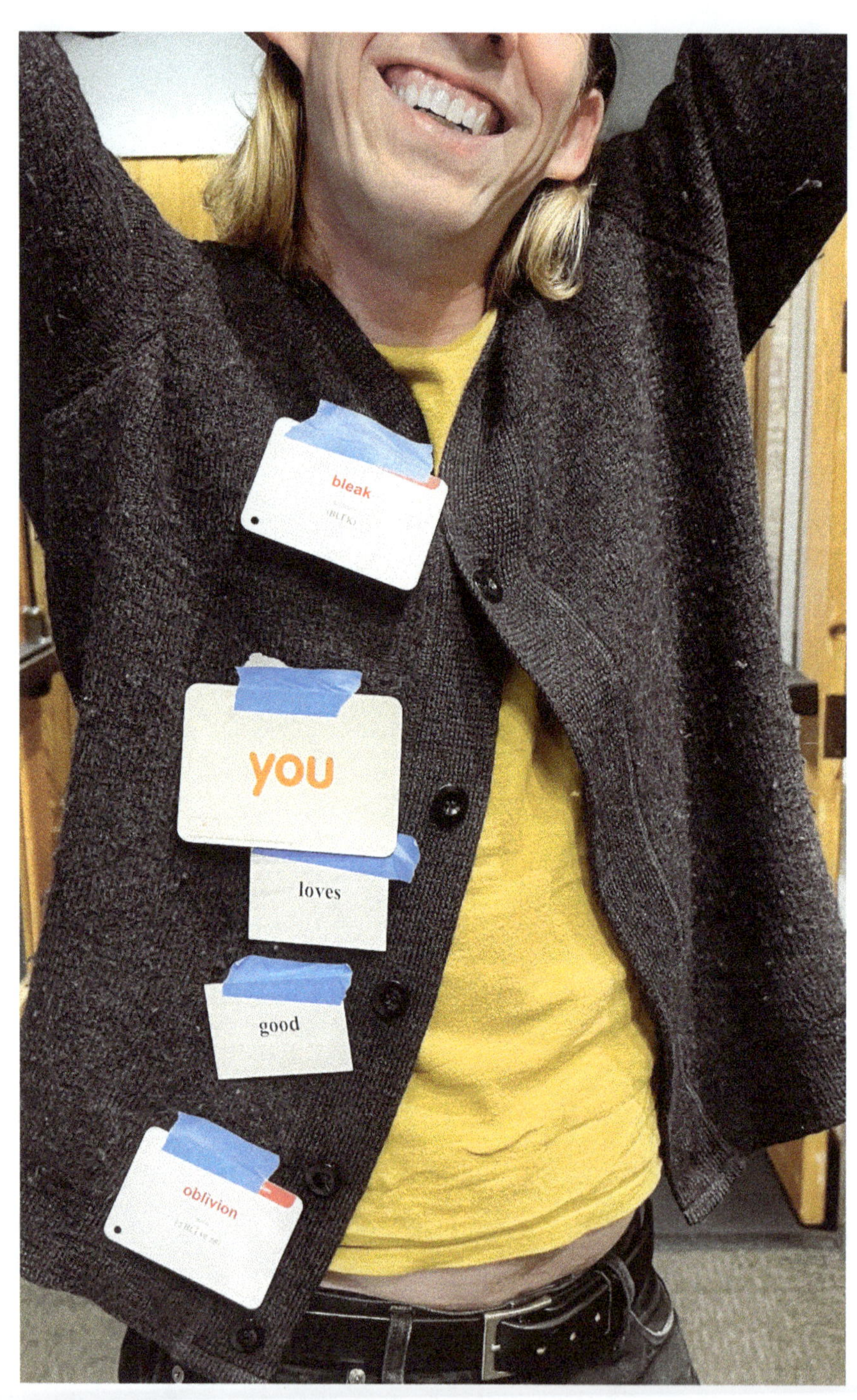

HUMAN MAGNETIC POETRY created by community members on Nov. 4, 2022 at First Matter Press's *Poetry Scramble.*

I MAKE THREE SEPARATE ATTEMPTS TO WRITE MY AMAZON.COM AUTHOR BIO

dan wiencek

I don't remember the city
where I was born only
blue shag carpet on the back
of my young neck

ascending into my crib
by stepping on my father's knee
watching my mother paint
a lamp in the shape of
a jack-in-the-box her brush
laying down stripes
of navy blue and '70s red

*Dan Wiencek remembers owning a pair of Mork suspenders and a Batman alarm clock
that spoke to him every morning. He knows these things are important but cannot explain
why. It would be so much easier if he could write songs, but he has no gift for melody. He
lives about as far away as he can get.*

the night I struck the floor
with my head I ran
like a wild thing
through the kitchen and halls
evading every arm until my father
finally caught me
my eyes tearing
under a ceiling fixture
while an ice cube melted
on my forehead

I once shared a bed
with a cousin who tried to convince me
to pull my underwear down
he would pretend to turn
into the Hulk because
he knew it scared me
to think of looking
in the mirror and seeing
white eyes stare back

Dan Wiencek writes poems fitfully, the way rain gradually carves new faces into old stone. He was born in some place named after a tree, which probably no longer exists except in his own memories. He doesn't speak to a single friend he made before he turned 15 and when he thinks of the past he instinctively squints, as though attempting to do math in his head. To talk about himself at even this length goes against his instincts.

the world that shaped us
dissolves into curbside grit
stores that became other stores
a slightly younger sun draping
warmth over our shoulders

I recall a body that hadn't learned
to stink or get erections in class
a mind just beginning to peek
out from under the blankets already
frightened of the wrong things

if you round the corner and
see him try to warn him
that the distance between
home and school shrinks
a little each time he walks it

Dan Wiencek is a series of excited quantum states, an unknowable number of asynchronous possibilities, any and all of which could accurately be described as real. He gives you permission to construct him in your mind and know that whatever conclusion you arrive at, you are correct.

Of "I Make Three Separate Attempts…": *Just as I've never been much for formal poetry, I've never been drawn to the idea of poems as tools of memoir. Writing explicitly about my own life doesn't hold much appeal to me. That said, it was in the process of introducing my book to the world that the dilemma captured in this piece emerged. I struggle with the idea that a reader might want or need to know anything about me in order to appreciate what I write, and I always groan when I hear poets elaborately introduce their own work before reading it. So this piece forces me to talk about myself in a direct manner I haven't really done before. We'll see how and when it happens again.*

DAN WIENCEK's poetry has appeared in publications that include *New Ohio Review, Sou'wester, The Briar Cliff Review* and *Carve*. His first collection of poems, *Routes Between Raindrops*, was published by First Matter Press in 2021. Born and raised in Illinois, he now lives with his wife in a large city in the Pacific Northwest.

ERASURE created by community members on Nov. 4, 2022 at First Matter Press's *Poetry Scramble*.

GENDER EUPHORIA

emily moon

I toured the castles
of crudité,
each with its knight
of assholery.

This one, a historic
haiku. That one,
a stormy kayak maven.
Another, a mere shout.

I'm doing the things
I set out to do:
I changed my clothes,
grew my boobs,
painted my lips.

I grew comfortable in my skin.
I move fluidly here
and there without a care.
I'm ma'amed and
she'd and her'd.

Now, men interrupt me,
talk down to me
talk over me,
treat me as if I'm not there,
and hold doors for me.

I have arrived!

THE DENVER PUBLIC LIBRARY

emily moon

Weldon steps out of the mist
into the pool of light on the corner,
taps a cigarette from an engraved case,
snaps his Zippo open,
and produces a cherry
at the end of the smoke.

He thinks about
the knotted routes
of his wayward existence.

His memory shifts to the back room
at the Denver Public Library,
times spent there with Norris,
the crackling electricity,
the scent of that place,
their mingled breaths.

Now, after all these years,
Norris waits for him
at a hotel bar.

He takes a drag,
ponders the meeting,
wonders what remains.
Is the excitement thumping his chest
anticipation anxiety?
Fear?

He tosses the butt to the gutter,
brushes his neatly trimmed moustache
with a forefinger,
and pulls his fedora to shade his eyes.
With a resolute smile,
he marches down the block
toward the light of the hotel.

Of "The Denver Public Library": *This poem continues the imagined journeys of Weldon Keys from* It's Just You & Me, Miss Moon.

EMILY MOON (she/her) is a transgender poet from Portland, Ore. She is author of *It's Just You & Me, Miss Moon.* Her work includes appearances in or forthcoming from *Pile Press, Boats Against the Current, The Viridian Door, Banyan Review, The Dawn Review, Culinary Origami,* and elsewhere. You can find her on Instagram @emilymoonpoet

VISITING GOYA

ahuva s. zaslavsky

After visiting the Prado for three days in a row, I head northeast on the train to Zaragoza. I sit in the aisle, watching the view past the passenger's shoulder. She is looking at her phone, indifferent to the outside swooshing at a high speed, but my eyes try to absorb the foreign sights. At the age of 57, it's a time of many firsts—leaving my country, getting on a plane, crossing an ocean—and now I'm in Spain on a Goya exploration.

Back home, I work at the city garbage center, where people with big trucks come to get rid of accumulated stuff they don't want anymore. I meet hoarders, gardeners, home-flippers, construction workers, young and old mourners, mid-life-new-chapter-openers, bankrupters, business owners and other ordinary humans—all flocking to the dump to dispose old and new materials, but also their memories and pain. Some even believe that leaving the place with an empty trunk will ease their tormented bodies and souls.

While trucks back up in reverse, beeping all the way to the rim of the enormous pile, I wait in the corner with my shopping cart, eyes wide open to catch what these metal mouths are about to spit out. When they are done, like a vulture, I pounce on my prey. Quickly rolling the cart to the fresh addition of trash and digging through, I find keepers. I work fast; by the time one truck pulls out, another is already in line.

Yes, this is what I do: I find valuable things in other people's junk. I spend my days in the bowels of the municipal dump, watching the monstrous mountain of trash devour, chew, shred and digest—always gurgling, never satisfied. You may consider my work inferior, but I think I am a savior. I decide what things will not end up in the landfill or the ocean! I restore value to abandoned objects! I rescue artifacts! I save materials from the abyss!

You ask what brought me to Spain. The simplest answer is: The dump. Or rather, a book I found in the dump. Many months ago, while digging in a black plastic bag, an image of a bloody monster clutching a man and chewing on his arm peeked through and I knew it needed to be saved. I am not an intellectual or anything like that, but since then I have learned everything possible about Francisco de Goya.

At the final stop, I get off and don't waste any time. The taxi heads to the city, and I can see the ancient Ebro and the towers of the Basilica rise high. The old city streets turn into narrow alleys and sunlight highlights the golden ocher of the buildings.

Unlike the Prado, where I dragged my tired feet along the magnificent corridors, Museo Goya is small. And surprisingly busy. As I walk towards the prints gallery I wonder how this space can contain all the disasters of war.

Although the images are well displayed—like an archive of historical documents—I feel disoriented. The rooms are completely dark and crammed with people. As I walk, I rub against moving bodies in the masterly silence reserved only to cemeteries. It is as if the piles of corpses from the images spilled into the room. I smell the humid breath of those passing by. Cold sweat trickles down my spine.

Is it because of the horrible captures in the prints or because it is hard to approach them due to the crowd, that I see no images, only dark stains? It is extremely unpleasant here. I am desperate to get out. Frantically I grab the show's catalog, push my body out of the gallery and burst back to the street, feeling as if I was excreted from hell. It is sorely bright, and I shield my eyes until adjusted to the day. There are still hours to kill before the train departs—I didn't anticipate finishing so early.

Disappointed with the shocking experience, I remember nothing came to my mouth today. Dizzy,

I walk towards Plaza de Pilar, hoping to find food. All the restaurants are packed and I can't find a table. I walk east towards the Cathedral del Salvador De Zaragoza in Plaza De la Seo. I think about Goya taking the same route. I find a deli and get in for something to eat. There is a display of pickles and olives. I have never seen olives so large, I think while loading a bag with stuffed black olives.

On a bench, I devour the huge olives. I stuff my mouth with them, surprised by how black they are. I imagine my mouth filled with dark salty juice. A group of teenagers skateboard on an improvised ramp, and I worry one will smash their arm.

I decide to enter the cathedral and find the place empty, its gold glow mesmerizing. I pass by saints and icons in the chapels trying to guess which one was a Goya. In a short time I shifted from the underworlds of war and death at the museum to exalted and holy heights here—both of which are man-made. I can't find solace in this tabernacle of the saints, and with a heartburn rising up my esophagus—from the excessive amount of black olives?—I plan to leave Zaragoza.

Before leaving the cathedral I spot a sign pointing up: Museo de Tapices. I decide to see what's there.

Many stairs lead to the tapestry museum and halfway up I am not sure I can continue. But, as if bewitched, my body carries me on. Across deep burgundy walls hang monumental tapestries, dated to the medieval period. I feel as if I have traveled back in time, and now am walking among castles, villages and sailing ships, while mythical creatures tell me stories of mystery and passion. I hover between the rooms where time doesn't exist, only eternal beauty and splendor.

On the train back to Madrid I fall asleep. I wake up from an amusing dream where in all of Goya's etchings there are hills made of black olives, dripping dark ink on marvelous tapestries. I don't worry about finding meaning in it. Instead, I am concerned about Monday and going back to work at the dump. I imagine the big trash pile and the countless black sealed bags we are not allowed to open because of what they might contain—one never knows what people want to get rid of—weapons, drugs, secrets, even dead bodies, or anything rotten. But my curiosity can never help itself, and I always carry a utility knife in my vest. And when my supervisor is not around, I slash open the bags and dig my hands deep into the filth. Who knows what treasures I might find?

AHUVA S. ZASLAVSKY lives and works in Portland, Oregon. She was born in Tel Aviv and graduated from The University of the Negev, Israel with a BA in behavioral sciences. ahuva completed her MFA in Visual Studies at the Pacific Northwest College of Art, earning the LR Visual Studies MFA Thesis Award. ahuva's multimedia works are examinations into the relationship of space and place to memory and trauma and have been shown locally and nationally. She has completed the Art/Lab Fellowship in 2022 and was named to GLEAN Portland's 2022 Artist Residency. ahuva is the author of *Between These Borders Wonders a Golem* (First Matter Press, 2022).

THE MILE LONG SCROLL

sara swoboda

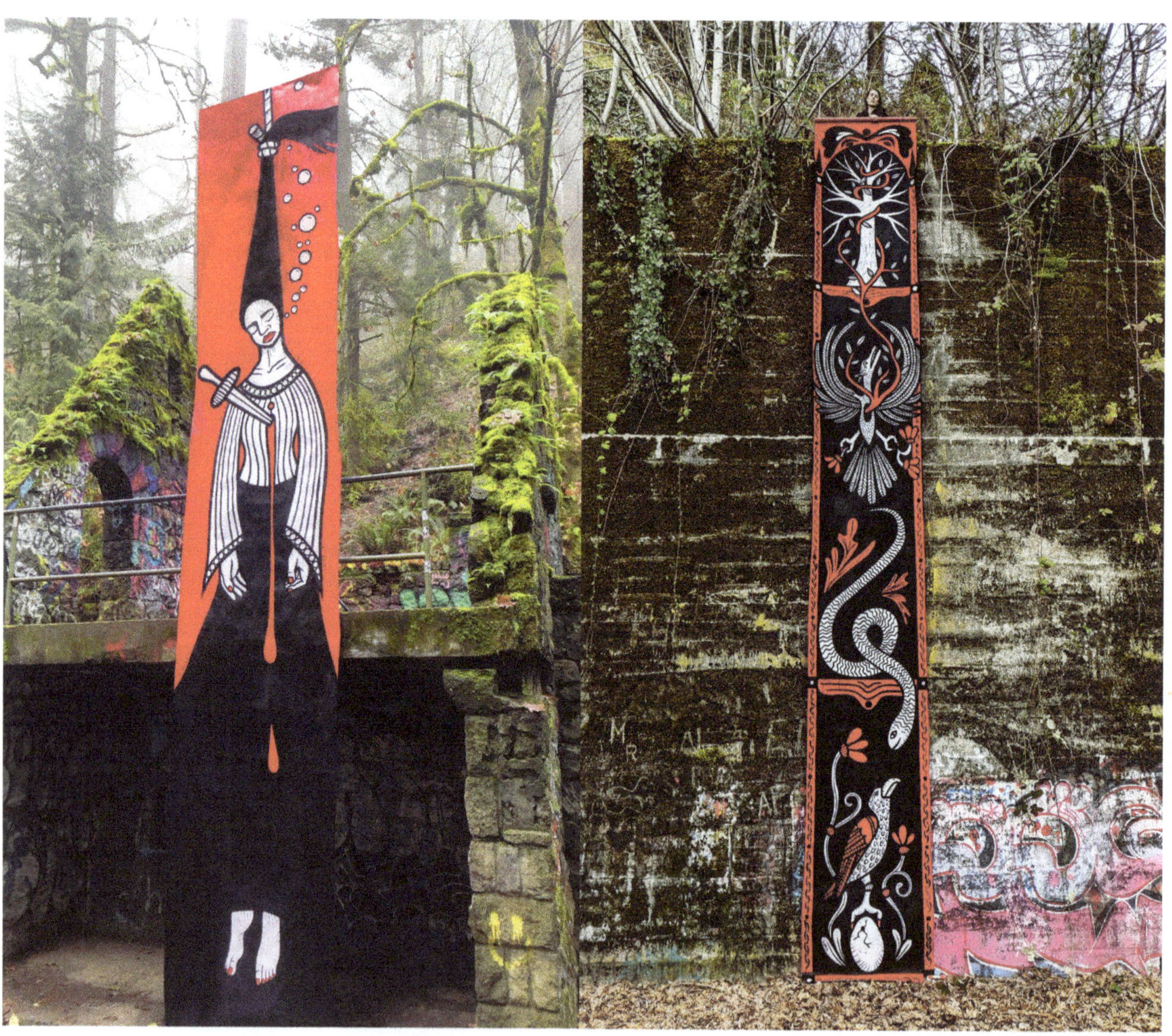

Of "The Mile Long Scroll": *An ambitious long-term project started in late 2019, The Mile Long Scroll is a four-foot-wide continuous roll of art that Sara Swoboda adds to every day, responding to current events and personal experiences of daily life. These images depict portions of the Mile Long Scroll made in 2020 and 2021. Sara continues to add to the scroll today.*

SARA SWOBODA has resided in Portland, Oregon since 2016. With a background of working in stop motion animation, her process is deeply influenced by narrative storytelling and experimentations with scale. She was First Matter Press's featured cover artist in 2020.

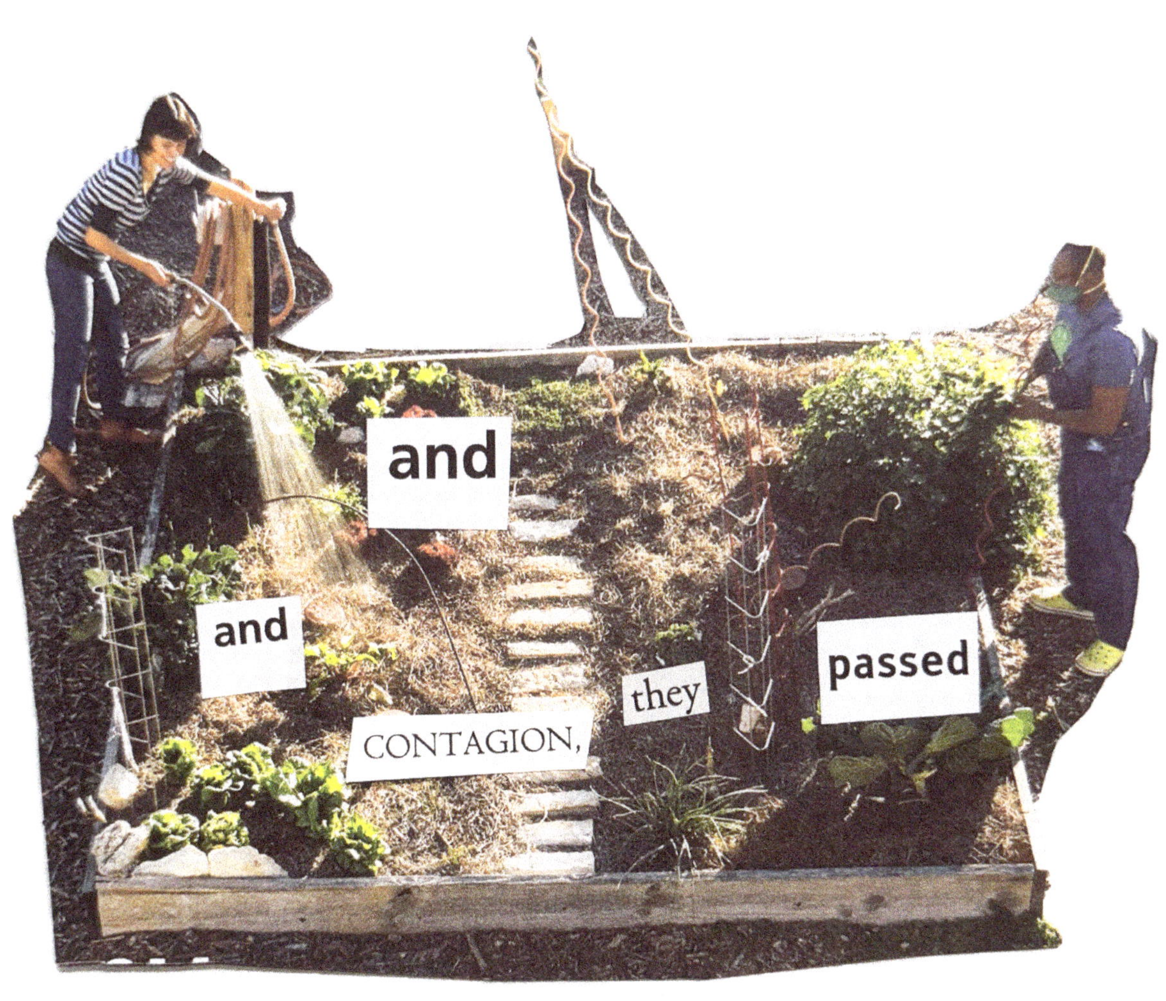

COLLAGE created by community members on November 4, 2022 at First Matter Press's *Poetry Scramble* (a Literary Arts' Portland Book Festival Cover to Cover event).

VULTURE WEDDING FUNERAL

rachel mulder

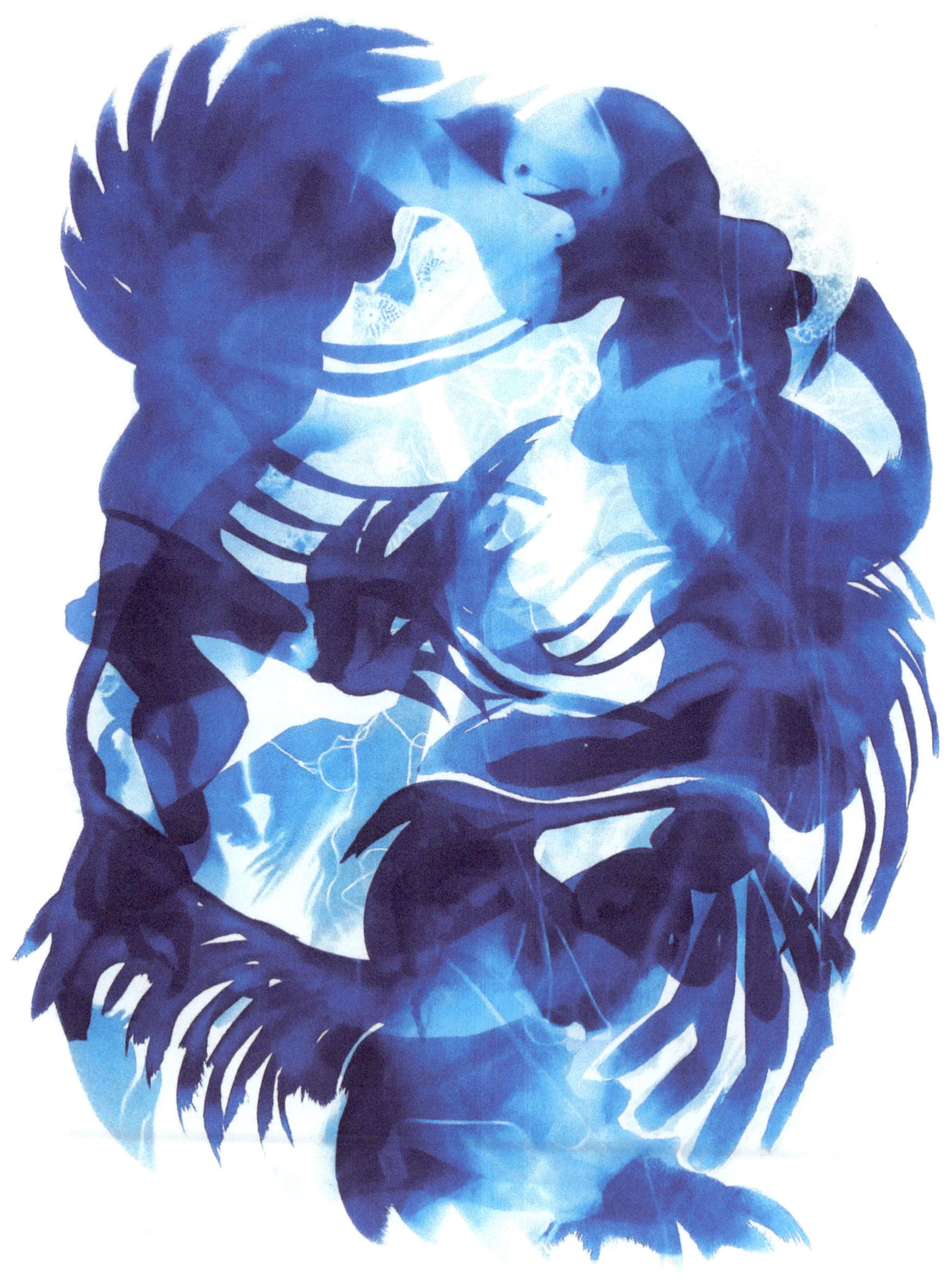

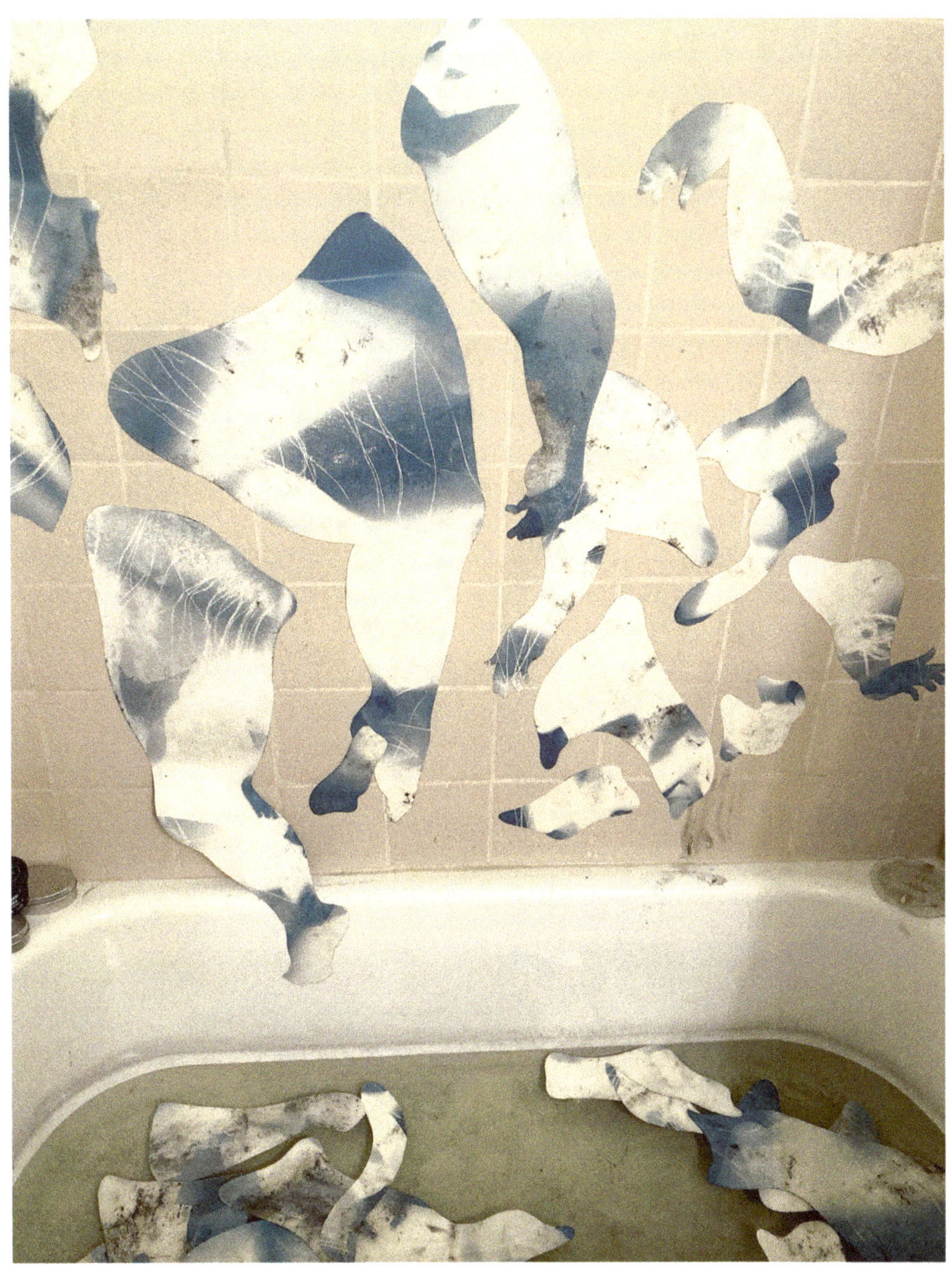

Of "Vulture Wedding Funeral" and the cyanotype process: *I'm so deeply excited about my experimental cyanotypes. I feel like I'm just starting to dig into this drawer-ly rhythm I've found within this alternative-photo process. I'm in love with the polarity of cyanotypes: on one hand it's a mundane, almost vulgar act: placing objects on paper in the sun, rinsing it in my bathtub, waiting to dry by the toilet. But what emerges is real transformation and surprise and this outrageous blue magic! While dreaming up ahuva s. zaslavsky's book cover for between these borders wanders a golem, we discovered that ahuva's writing and both of our visual artworks explored many parallel themes—the grotesque, bodies, constructing and destructing, transformation. Cyanotypes lend themselves so beautifully to my current creative desires and were featured in our two-person show in the summer of 2023, transmogrified, which came to be because of our meeting in the 2022 First Matter Press Cohort!*

RACHEL MULDER lives in Portland, Oregon, with her two cats, Opal and Tomasina. She was born in rural Wisconsin and when she was small she spent a lot of time sitting in the grass staring, obsessing about animals, drooling over the nastiness of cartoons, and peeling her skin off. She vacillates between obsessive and loosey-goosey ways of working but refers to it all as Drawing. She explores many types of media, including water-soluble graphite, pen and ink, cyanotype, and her wet hair on the shower wall. She earned her BFA in print-making at the Milwaukee Institute of Art & Design in 2009, and though she indulges in the one-of-a-kind-ness of drawings, the images she makes are often tinged with a longing for printmaking in texture and feeling.

A STRANGER CAME TO TOWN

jessica e. pierce

> *All great literature is one of two stories; a man goes on a journey or a stranger comes to town.*
> —Tolstoy

I was confused as he looked just like my husband
but said he wasn't. I did believe him
as I'd seen him walk down the street,
and I was sure I'd seen my husband
in the house earlier.

I went to look for my husband
just to make sure I wasn't going crazy.
I wanted to have the two of them stand
next to each other and see if
they really were doppelgangers
or if I was missing something.

But he wasn't in any of his usual spots—
the kitchen table, the bathroom,
deep in a cocoon of sleep
wishing he lived a different life.
The stranger sat quietly
as I leaned against the doorway
and studied his face.
Then he got up and left.

The threshold whispered
you can wake up now.
He's gone.
This is your life.

Of "A stranger came to town": *This poem leans more than much of my earlier work on a seemingly straightforward narrative of observation, while also tapping into the power of the volta at the end, without offering too much resolution.*

I HAVE STOPPED LOVING YOU

jessica e. pierce

And am amazed at how much else
I still love, love more, even.
This includes my mother, my own hands
on my own body, and crows.
A student tells me a story about a woman
who fed a raucous murder every day,
despite the eye rolls of neighbors grumbling
they're well fed enough as it is.
One morning she slipped, and the crows
would not leave her fallen, raised such hell
no one could ignore them, or her.
And sometimes this is how saving goes.

Of "I have stopped loving you": *This poem continues* Consider the Body, Winged's *(First Matter Press, 2021) exploration of my own constellated body and turns unflinchingly into the dissolution of my marriage.*

JESSICA E. PIERCE's debut collection, *Consider the Body, Winged*, was published by First Matter Press in 2021. Her poems have appeared in *Bellingham Review, Tar River Poetry, Euphony, Northwest Review, JMWW, Slushpile, Writer Mother Monster*, and elsewhere. A semi-finalist and two-time finalist for the Pablo Neruda Prize from *Nimrod*, she's been a two-time finalist for the Lois Cranston Memorial Poetry Prize from *CALYX*, as well as a finalist for the *New Ohio Review*'s NORward Prize and the MVICW Poetry Contest, for which she received a Poet Fellowship. Jessica earned her Ed.M. from Harvard and works in a large school district in Oregon to create anti-racist alternatives to exclusionary discipline.

So why can't I let it go?!

Something about hormones + magnets
+ what we add + adorn to remake ourselves
we slip on in the morning and off again at night, like a smile
slipping into the siren call of "later", letting it sooth aching cheeks
Sour tinges pucker lips
        surprise draws tears from open eyes
        You are a tender thing

        with three glass eyes

EXQUISITE CORPSE written by community members on Nov. 4, 2022 at First Matter Press's *Poetry Scramble*. Starting line "So why can't I let it go?" was excerpted from *Between These Borders Wanders a Golem* by ahuva s. zaslavsky (First Matter Press, 2022).

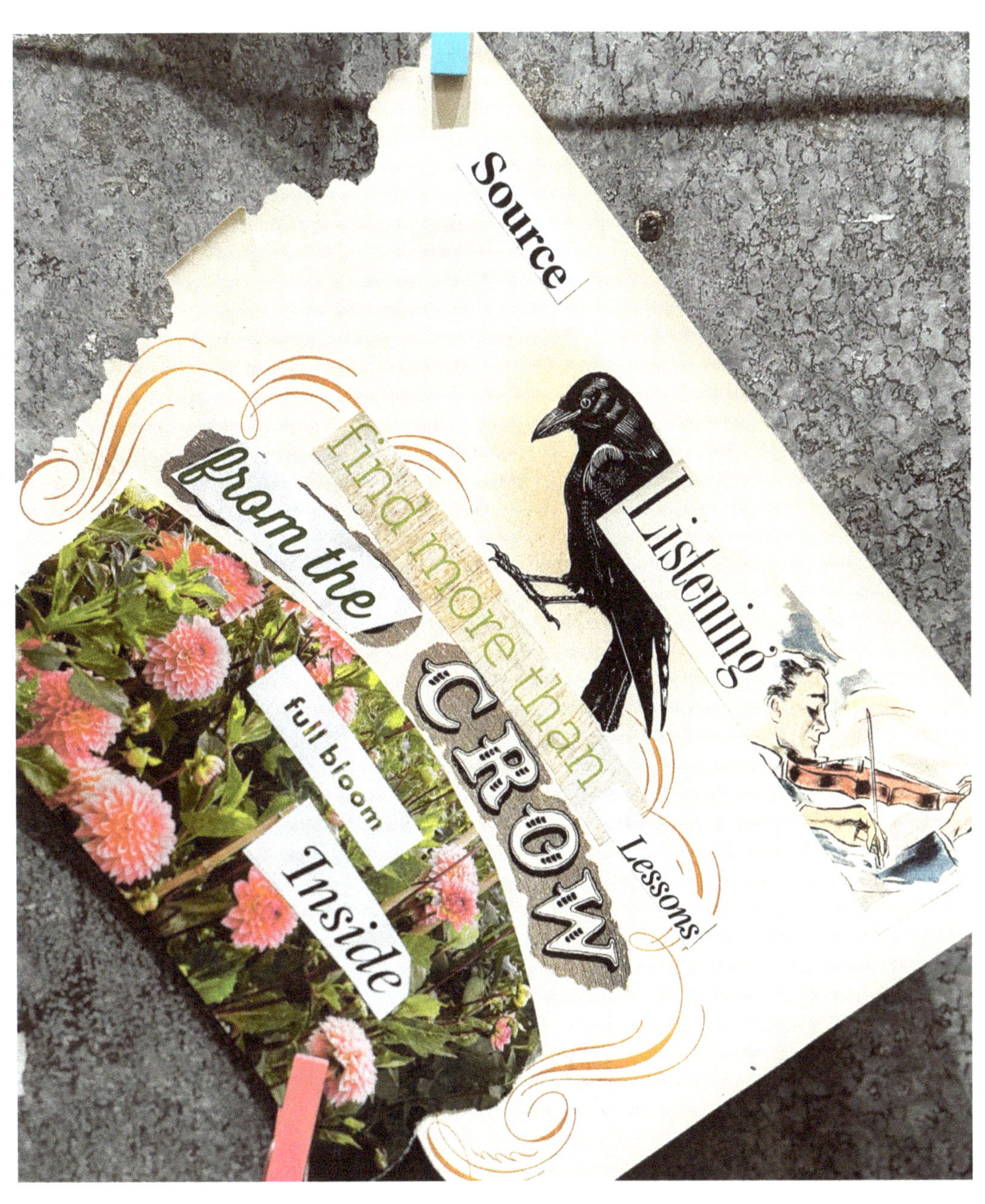

COLLAGE created by community members on Nov. 4, 2022 at First Matter Press's *Poetry Scramble*.

INTRODUCTION

hailey spencer

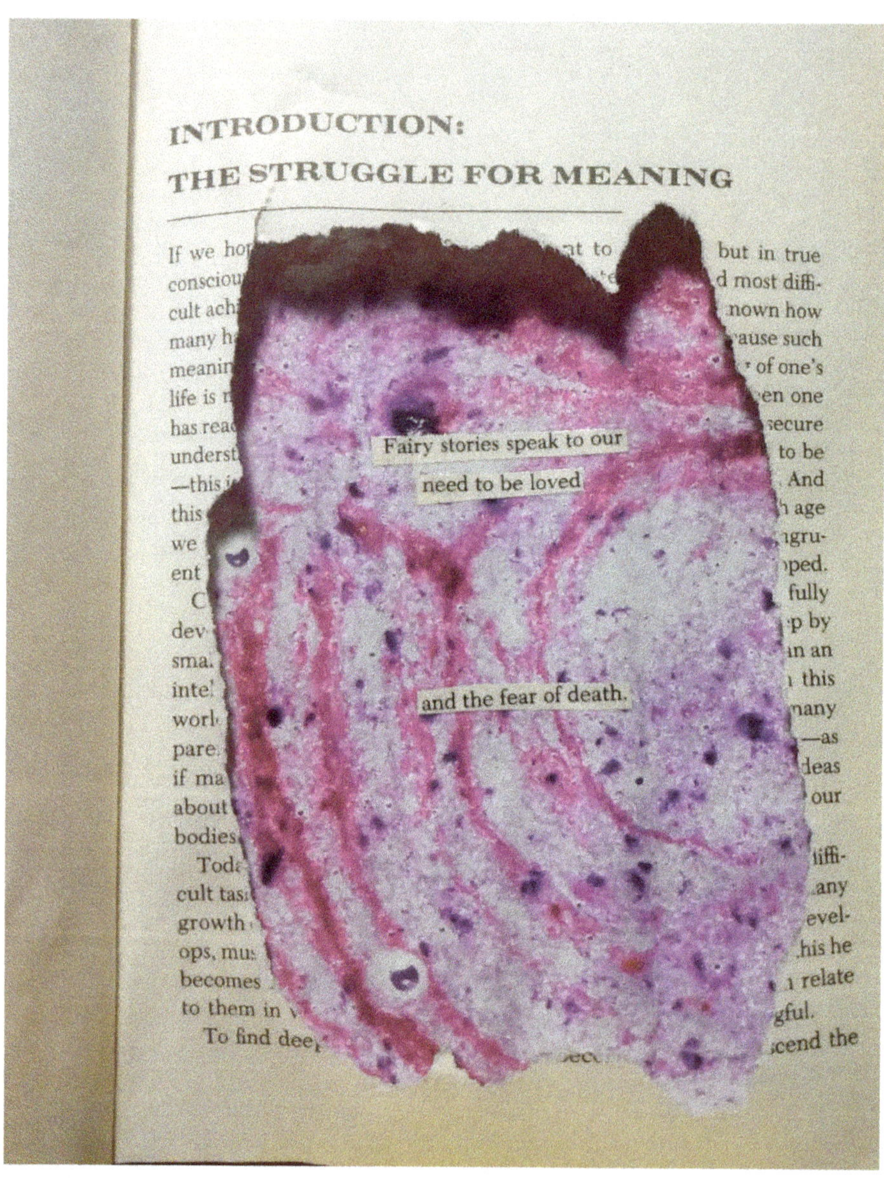

Of "Introduction," "Snow White" & "Acknowledgements": Bruno Bettelheim's The Uses of Enchantment is considered on of the quintessential folklore texts. In it, the author analyzes popular fairy tales using a Freudian lens. In particular, he focuses on the meaning that children may derive from fairy tales, based on childhood stages of the psyche. In 1977, it received a National Book Award in the Contemporary Thought category.

It is also an incredibly controversial work of scholarship.
Aside from fellow folklorist Alan Dundes' accusations that Bettelheim plagiarized much of the text, Bettelheim has also been accused of misrepresenting his credentials. In The Great Cat Massacre, Robert Darnton argues that Bettelheim's writing on folklore ignores the historical context in which these stories were told. Bettelheim is also controversial outside the world of folklore, especially for his theories on autism, which I will not explain in detail here as it falls outside the scope of this project.

Knowing all of this already, I bought a copy of The Uses of Enchantment at a used bookstore while working on Stories for When the Wolves Arrive. There are several reasons for this. One was curiosity. Another was the need to understand something

SNOW WHITE

hailey spencer

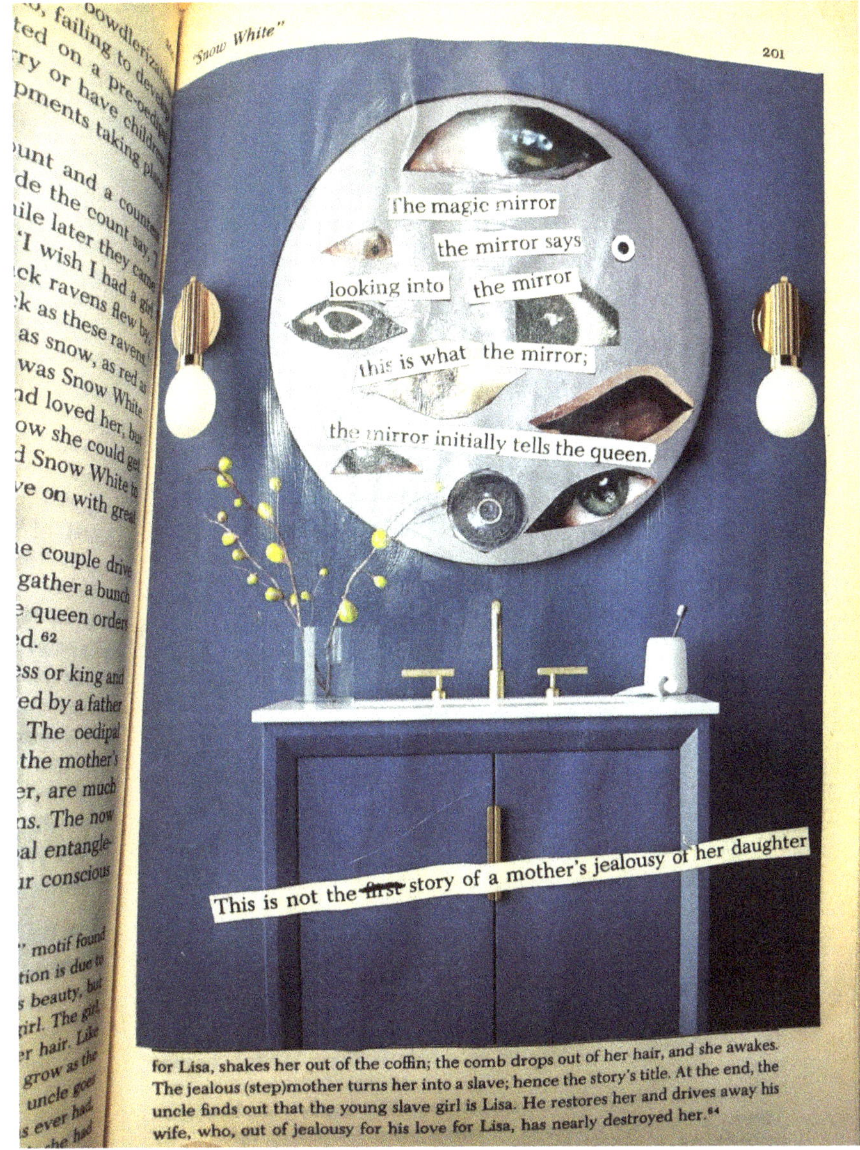

before arguing so wholly against it. A distant friend who took a folklore class had been assigned the book, so I knew it was still being used in academic spaces. I also thought, perhaps, there would be some items of interest, even in the midst of all I knew to be wrong with the book.

In the name of full disclosure, I will tell you now that I did not finish the book. Working on my Rapunzel poems, I read approximately half of Bettelheim's chapter on Rapunzel and had to dismiss the book entirely. In his whole psychosexual analysis of the Grimm version of Rapunzel, he did not one single time cite the Grimm's 1812 manuscripts, in which Rapunzel's deceit is discovered by the witch because her pregnant belly can no longer fit into her dresses. This would have strengthened his argument considerably, and yet, he only used the better-known 1857 versions of the stories. I no longer trusted his scholarship enough to read further.

And yet, I still owned a copy of this book.

I don't know that I ever expect to understand Bettelheim, but he has influenced the field of folklore heavily enough that I still

ACKNOWLEDGEMENTS

hailey spencer

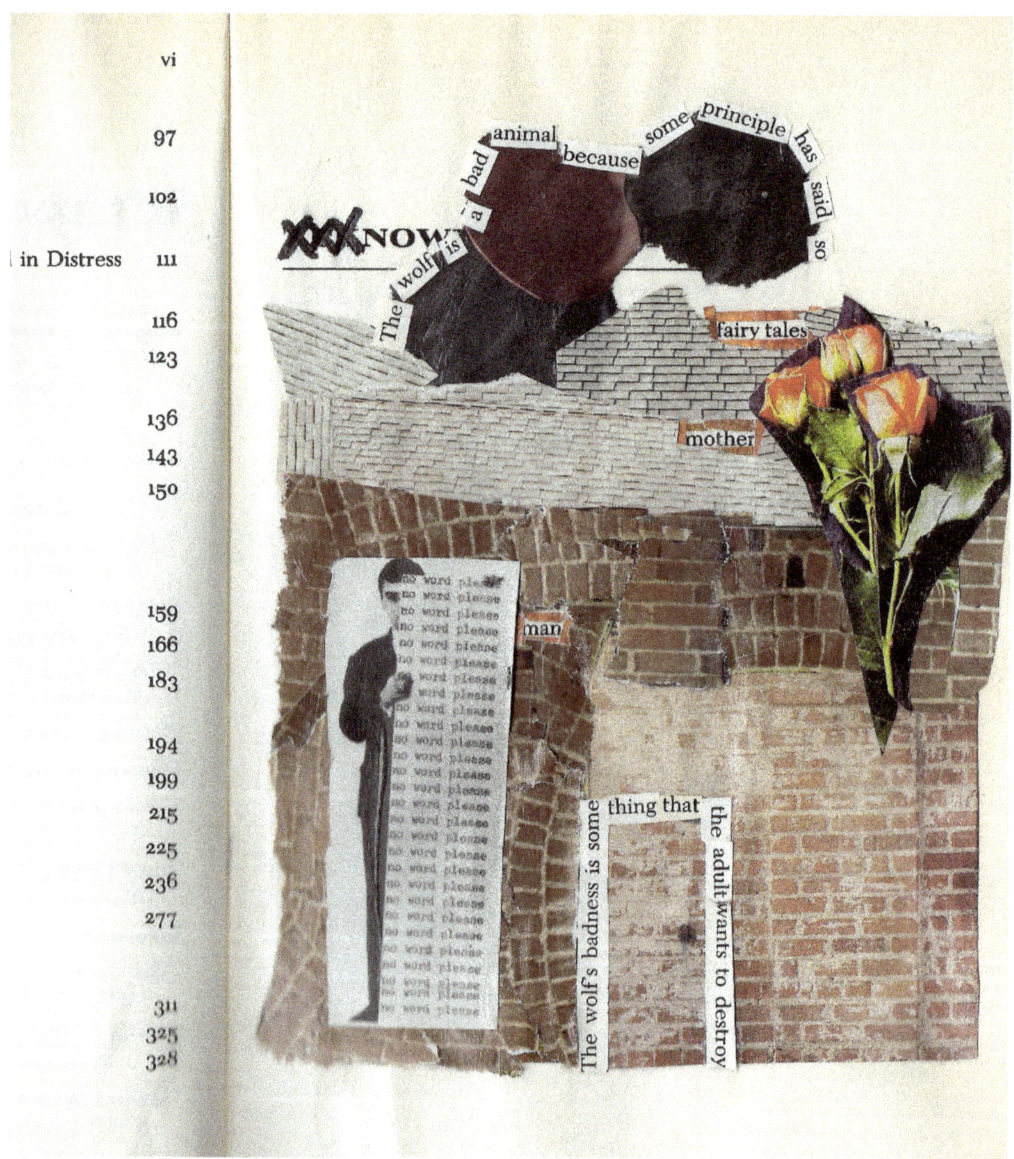

feel some need to understand it. I couldn't just set the book aside, so I've chosen a different way to explore it, one that allows me to insert my own thoughts into his text.

Folktales, by definition, are stories that have been passed around through many different people across place and time. This collage project is my attempt to understand my own relationship with Bettelheim's theories. Through the cutting out of pages and words, I've been forced to dig deeper into what he says, and where my own thoughts on the stories lie.

HAILEY SPENCER is, in the words of her wife Elizabeth, an absolute cloud of a girl. She is obsessed with fairy tales, and has an equally passionate rivalry with ants. Her first poetry collection, *Stories for When the Wolves Arrive*, was published in September 2022, followed by her chapbook *Out of Love in Spring* in October 2022. She lives and writes in Seattle, Washington. For more on Hailey and her work, visit haileyspencerwrites.com

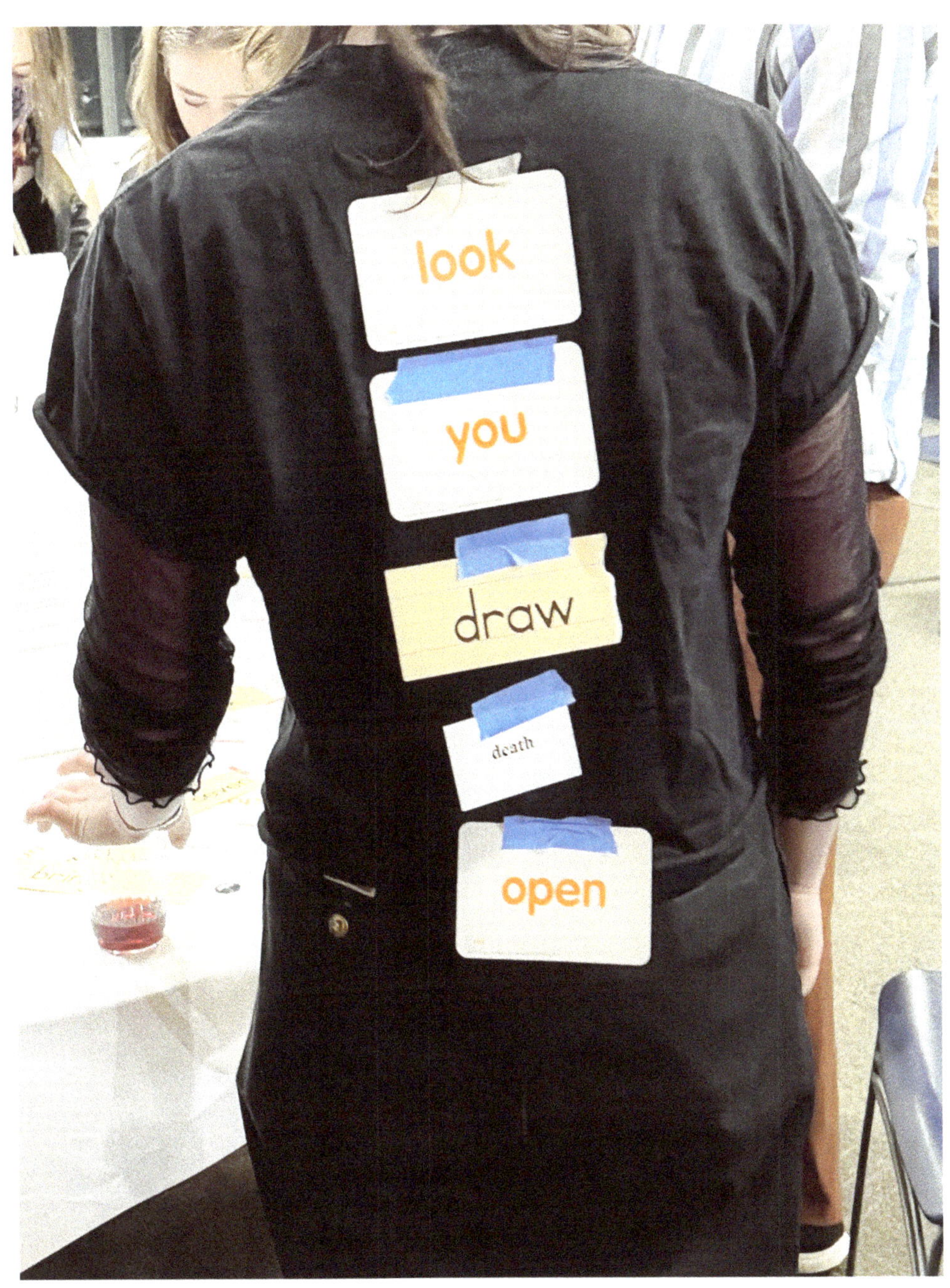

HUMAN MAGNETIC POETRY created by community members on Nov. 4, 2022 at First Matter Press's *Poetry Scramble*.

MY NEED YOUR NEED, A CENTO

ash good

*—in collaboration with Meredith Adelaide, Beth Melnick, Andra Vltavín,
Emily Vltavín & ahuva s. zaslavsky*

1.

capricious inner compass / in the train station in paris / guesses the nationality of
women's asses / it is hard to predict / lineage amnesia / a thick lagoon off an old
road / chasing after a blue plastic ball

2.

my need your need / motion for the sharks / the fight to maintain eyes wide / a string
along the upper edge / conditioned to jump / an instinctive calculation / to remain
untouchable

3.

the violent way of creating a flower / to be revealed is to be dissolved / there is such
distance between myself & who i thought i was / and yet light and heat / the sun is
captured / as if memorizing the order of nature / we have to ask who imagines this

4.

when i remember it is like a sip of mezcal / i just want to invite you to a lava flow /
of sloppy love / leaping blue in that fall / look upon each other / somehow fuming
& aligning / we could do it & still survive

LIBERATION, A CENTO

ash good

—in collaboration with Sam Cimino, Gabby Hancher, Jenn Lalime, Sierra Vida Lisa, Holaday Mason, Beth Melnick, Dawn Thompson, Andra Vltavín & ahuva s. zaslavsky

hands burn hot with magic / bodies speak only truth / the quiet black core / whispers
at all hours / the bones know / i long daily / don't look at me through that flame / maybe
drunk maybe needing water or food / we talk now via psychic connection / somedays
i want to lay my body over everything / you do not scare me—you never have / i guess
that's it—the gift or whatever / the skin of the night / is so soft / my naked shoulders /
gathering our ghosts / i want to fly & that requires / breaking into the room of my
dream / freedom in loose hair

Of "my need your need, a cento" & "liberation, a cento": *While attending online generative writing circles and poetry readings during the early pandemic, I began a listening practice of capturing a few gut-punch lines which I'd combine into brief collages of the collective energy we'd shared during that gathering. Playing with language in this way continues to transform how I approach line by line composition in my own poems.*

ASH GOOD (they/them) is the author of *us clumsy gods* (What Books Press, 2022) & four previous poetry collections. They are cofounding editor of First Matter Press, a nonprofit writer collective based in Portland, OR. Their poetry has been nominated for Best of the Net & appears in *Faultline, Cimarron Review, 45th Parallel, Chautauqua, Bird Coat Quarterly, Voicemail Poems* & others. www.ashgood.com

—AFTER (A CHAIN REACTION)

andra vltavín, caroline wilcox reul, ash good & lauren paredes

1.

DEAR COUNTRY

Elisabeth Borchers (translated by Caroline Wilcox Reul)

Stop
And think, I told myself.
And I think:
By day by night, you're worth only
Half as much, look at the
Chaos of your flip sides
Frenzied, thorough and
Conductive—that's you.
You've never been afraid,
Not even of
Yourself.

Of "—After (A Chain Reaction)": *We are four poets and translators who find that writing in community both encourages more prolific writing and adds life to what we write. This is an excerpt from a cycle of response poems, similar to the children's game "Telephone," that we engaged in between 2018 and 2020. We jumped off with a member's translation of the Elisabeth Borchers' poem, "Dear Country." One member wrote an initial response poem and sent it to the next member, who then wrote a response to that poem. That poet then sent it off to a third member and so forth, round and round, alternating the poet to whom we respond each time. Each poet only read the preceding poem in this process.*

The initial poem, however, was known to everyone and provided the themes for the response collection as a whole. We each considered the dichotomies of both the external and internal worlds: the body and its membrane-thin border to the outer world, the day and night of the soul, the "flipsides" of our multiplicitous identities.

We watch our work expand, overlap, and diverge, only to converge and complement each other again. It is a journey that provides a concrete example of the commonality of human experience and how frequently we affect each other, often unknowingly.

"Dear Country" from Who Lives by Elisabeth Borchers, translated by Caroline Wilcox Reul (Tavern Books, 2017) is reprinted with permission.

2.

SOUNDBATH OF SELF

Andra Vltavín

She looks at you when she says, *pull all your selves back;*
there is room for each of them.

She says you can hold
each of your thousand names,

and you wonder
if you will ever have that many

or if they are even necessary.
Her name rings in your head and silences

a second freight train. Its vibrations again remind you
you are human.

Beneath these sounds, you see a doe with one of your eyes,
then a collage of painted mouths becomes

a mass of female bodies until a dozen tiny hands
gently peer into the expanse

of vulva and what you do not believe
pours in through this fleshy portal. These hands,

bodies, lips, eyes are not yours but everyone's
sitting around the hearth where you are whole,

humming *home.*

ANDRA VLTAVÍN (formerly K. M. Lighthouse) is the author of *Body Until Light*, *Time Counts Backward from Infinity*, and two chapbooks of poetry. They have been published in many journals, including *Toasted Cheese*, and were a winner of the 2021 DiBiase poetry contest. They live the revolutions of queerness, creative reuse, and polyamory with their wife, two bunnies, and a spinning wheel in Portland, OR. (FMP Editor, 2018–22)

3.

LEXICON OF AN IDIOLECT

Caroline Wilcox Reul

and I know zest of life is laced with toxins
and nutrients I bake into a cake called

                                                 hunger

you called me mother before that was my name
and then I knew how to say it.
and "home" means

                                                 home

and "body" means

                                                 body

but "find" means *look*
and "country" means *elsewhere*
and "here" means *melting pot*
and "melting pot" means *depart.*
you won't tell me where I am, toes knees belly cheek,
you won't respond when I ask you how to say

                                             comfort

which means "longing" and

                                             respite

which is hard to translate.
you won't answer when I ask you
how you say "still."

CAROLINE WILCOX REUL is a translator, lexicographer and occasionally she writes a poem. Her poetry translations can be found in the *PEN Poetry Series, Lunch Ticket, The Los Angeles Review, The Michigan Quarterly Review, Your Impossible Voice, Tupelo Quarterly,* and others. (FMP Editor, 2021–22)

4.

WHAT IS THIS PRESSURE?

ash good

taste—turmeric—taste—sunshine—taste—parrot squawk
touch—branch scraping breast—touch—fountain—taste—oracle
card—hear—skin rubs—see—velvet pillow—a nymph is in
the garden—a bride is in the pool—a home sits fresh, unlived in
& locked—new life requires filing all the right paperwork
just ask—even after each tile is chosen & set—every faucet installed
after the unopened spare bottles from last week's christening are put in
out of the sun—you will be asked to wait—you will not want to be still
or might also find yourself patient—fingers tumbling in runes
unconcerned with fortune—the porcupine is docile if approached
correctly—only wants to play—you only hurt because you are scared—ask
this will be the year you will catch fear whole in your palms—swallow it all
what it comes to is you have nothing left to defend—if you want peace
don't discuss how you define these words differently—mistranslation
is not in the sound but underneath this tribal dialect—the silence may be
dishonest & you will know on eye contact—the world is as it is—just ask

ASH GOOD (they/them) is the author of *us clumsy gods* (What Books Press, 2022) & four previous poetry collections. They are cofounding editor of First Matter Press, a nonprofit writer collective based in Portland, OR. Their poetry has been nominated for Best of the Net & appears in *Faultline, Cimarron Review, 45th Parallel, Chautauqua, Bird Coat Quarterly, Voicemail Poems* & others. www.ashgood.com (FMP Editor, 2018–Present)

5.

I BELIEVE I WILL HOLD THE KEY

Lauren Paredes

If asked to describe the composition
          of a wholly-good moment
once disbelief has peacefully dismissed
          itself from the presence of 'blessing'
if that is too heavy-handed of a phrase
          let us consider 'underneath possibility'
invisible riches that can be palmed
          unscared of the way you will push
& pull at its mystery, like approaching
          familiar hurt & not feeling sting
finally there is no urgency to meaning-making
          knead too long & something will ruin
if asked to be more specific, open yourself
          to the power of a declined invitation
a garden gate pried open, see this silence
          for what it is: sunlight behind breast

LAUREN PAREDES is a storyteller across mediums with a soft spot for the unusual. Her work has appeared in *Salamander*, *TRNSFR*, *Warm Milk*, *phoebe*, and elsewhere. Her first chapbook of poems, *Otherwise, Magic*, was released in 2019 by First Matter Press. She currently resides in the Berkshires, nestled between hills. (FMP Editor, 2018–Present)

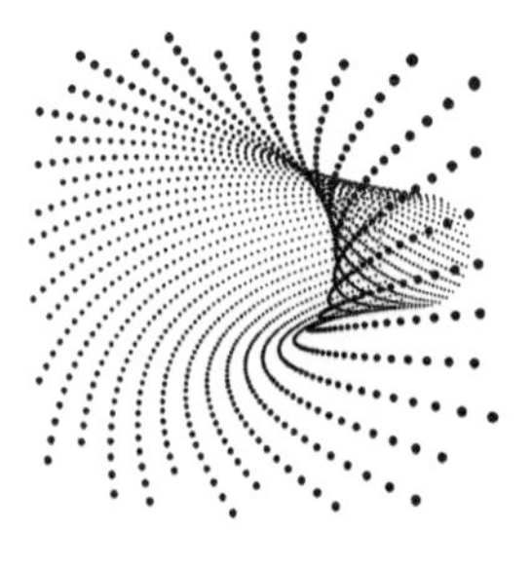

FIRSTMATTERPRESS

Portland, Ore.

First Matter Press is a writers' collective in Portland, Oregon, founded in 2018 to dissolve publication barriers for first-time publishing poets and genre-expanding writers. We invite authors into a creative cohort to crystallize manuscripts in dialogue with editors and fellow writers and collaborate with featured artists on original cover art. We are a 501(c)(3) non-profit organization and our authors maintain 100% of book sale proceeds. Please support independent booksellers by shopping for our titles at Bookshop.org

2023
FEATURED COVER ARTIST LARA ROUSE

FLOATING BONES
rae diamond

TEN-CENT FLOWER & OTHER TERRITORIES
charity e. yoro

OUR FAVORITE PEOPLE IN THE ROOM
edited by ash good, lauren paredes & emily moon

2022
FEATURED COVER ARTIST RACHEL MULDER

BETWEEN THESE BORDERS WANDERS A GOLEM
ahuva s. zaslavsky

EVEN THE AIR, TOO HEAVY
riley danvers

ONE ROW AFTER / BIR SIRA SONRA
sonya wohletz

SOMEONE I CAN HOLD GENTLY
xylophone mykland

STORIES FOR WHEN THE WOLVES ARRIVE
hailey spencer

9 781958 600078